Building Self-Esteem:

A Guide to Achieving Self-Acceptance

& a Healthier, Happier Life

By Megan MacCutcheon, M.Ed., LPC

Building Self-Esteem:
A Guild to Achieving Self-Acceptance
& a Healthier, Happier Life

Published by
Balancing Project Press, LLC
www.thebalancingproject.com

First Edition September 2014
Printed in the United States of America

ISBN-13: 978-0-9904134-0-0

Library of Congress Control Number: 2014918225

Disclaimer
The information in this book is not intended to provide medical advice and is sold with the understanding that the author is not liable for the misconception or misuse of information provided. The ideas and suggestions contained in this book are not intended as a substitute for consulting with a mental or medical health professional. If expert assistance, counseling, or therapy is needed, the services of a competent professional should be sought.

I dedicate this book to all of my clients and workshop participants, who bravely allow me to share their journeys and who continuously remind me of the importance of maintaining healthy self-esteem.

Special thanks to my husband for his support and patience as I was working on this project; to my sister for proofreading; to my editor for all her help in catching my typos and making useful suggestions; to the publishers and authors who have granted me permission to share their work throughout this book; and to my friend & mentor who encouraged me to publish this work.
Thank you!

Table of Contents

Forward

Dear Reader,

I'm so glad you picked up a copy of this workbook, and I sincerely hope it helps you to improve your quality of life. For the past several years, I have been teaching a Building Self-Esteem workshop and recently decided to compile the tools and ideas covered in the five-session course into a workbook so that workshop participants, as well as others, can continue to reference the information and work through chapters at their own pace.

The feedback I've received from workshop participants and my clients regarding the material has been overwhelmingly positive. One of the most common comments I hear during workshops is, "I wish we learned this stuff in grade school." I wholeheartedly agree. These concepts are something we all should learn at a young age. Instead, many of us wind up learning these things only after we find ourselves in a tough spot, facing difficult circumstances, challenging situations, or painful emotions that lead us to ultimately seek help and pursue change.

The concepts included are not new, and most are not my original ideas. They are things I've learned, collected, and borrowed from various resources over the years. References are cited throughout the workbook and in a Recommended Reading section at the end. I encourage you to check out these resources for even more information and greater understanding. Many ideas seem quiet simplistic; however, they are easier said than done. Implementing many of the tools recommended in this workbook involves breaking long-term habits. This requires commitment and a dedicated effort, but it is possible. You get what you put into practicing these tools. I encourage you to be patient with yourself as you learn new ideas, challenge old habits, and begin creating a better lifestyle.

In addition to this workbook, I have also created *Building Self-Esteem: A Guide to Achieving Self-Acceptance & a Healthier, Happier Life – Journal Companion.* The journal provides preliminary questions to review and consider before reading each chapter in this book and gives you a space to further explore topics covered as they relate to your own individual journey. It provides thought-provoking questions and inspirational quotes to encourage you as you work to build self-esteem.

In general, my workshop participants have been adult females and the pronouns and examples used throughout this workbook tend to be geared toward a feminine perspective; however, the ideas and tools are useful for anyone, both males and females, children, adolescents, and adults. If you are a man reading this book, please excuse the heavy use of feminine pronouns and references (especially in the chapter on body image) and know that the concepts for building self-esteem apply to you, too. The same tools useful in building self-esteem can also help individuals to decrease depression, manage anxiety, and feel better and more fulfilled overall.

I am so grateful to each client I have worked with and to each person who has taken my workshop over the past several years. These individuals have had the courage to share with me their personal struggles and to ask the insightful and thought-provoking questions that have inspired much of this workbook. The discussions I've had during workshops, coupled with the demonstration of immense progress I've witnessed in clients, is what made me believe publishing this workbook would be worthwhile.

Maybe you are one of my current clients or workshop participants, or maybe you stumbled upon the book some other way. Regardless, I encourage you to take from it the tools you need and find helpful, and to view building and maintaining self-esteem as a continuous endeavor. I wish you the best of luck on your journey to find self-acceptance and a healthier, happier life!

Sincerely,

Megan MacCutcheon

1

Assessments Pre-Tests

The following assessments can be useful to measure where you are starting out with self-esteem today. Fill them out according to how you feel and what you believe about yourself in the present moment. This will help give you a baseline regarding your current level of self-esteem and may provide an indication of which areas you need to focus on the most. At the end of the book, you will have the opportunity to retake the assessments to see whether any changes have occurred since learning new information and putting into practice various self-esteem-building tools.

Building and maintaining healthy self-esteem is an ongoing, lifelong process. While you probably will not see a complete 180 in scores from the pre-tests to the post-tests, you will likely notice some improvements and see shifts in various areas. As you continue to put the tools in this guide into practice moving forward, you will ultimately establish and build a foundation of healthy self-esteem.

The process of maintaining self-esteem is never over. Rather, it is something we must keep in mind and continue practicing throughout our lives. Building healthy self-esteem is vital, as self-esteem impacts all areas of your life, including mood, relationships, career, and level of success in various endeavors. These inventories can help give you a check-in regarding how you are doing.

In his book *Ten Days to Self-Esteem,* David Burns, M.D., provides inventories on depression, anxiety, and relationship satisfaction. These assessments can also be useful, and I encourage you to check out the book and track your progress with these assessments as well, since self-esteem can affect all of these areas of your life. Self-esteem and mental health issues, such as depression and anxiety, often go hand in hand. Self-esteem can play a role in whether you feel happy and fulfilled, and it can affect your relationships with others, both in terms of the people you choose to associate with and how healthy and happy your relationships are.

⁓∞⌐

Please complete the following assessments and save your scores in order to refer back to them and make comparisons to your scores on post-test assessments.

Self-Esteem Scale[*]

	Strongly Agree	Agree	Disagree	Strongly Disagree
1.) I feel that I am a person of worth, at least on an equal plane with others.				
2.) I feel that I have a number of good qualities.				
3.) All in all, I am inclined to feel that I am a failure.				
4.) I am able to do things as well as most other people.				
5.) I feel I do not have much to be proud of.				
6.) I take a positive attitude toward myself.				
7.) On the whole, I am satisfied with myself.				
8.) I wish I could have more respect for myself.				
9.) I certainly feel useless at times.				
10.) At times I think I am no good at all.				

Rosenberg's Self-Esteem Scale Scoring:

Scores are calculated as follows:

For items 1, 2, 4, 6, and 7:

Strongly Agree = 3
Agree = 2
Disagree = 1
Strongly Disagree = 0

For items 3, 5, 8, 9, and 10:

Strongly Agree = 0
Agree = 1
Disagree = 2
Strongly Disagree = 3

The scale ranges from 0 – 30. Scores between 15 and 25 are within normal range. Scores below 15 suggest low self-esteem.

The Self-Esteem Review[*]

Directions: Review the following statements. Rate how much you believe each statement, from 1 to 5. The highest rating, 5, means that you think the statement is completely true; 0 means that you completely *do not* believe the statement.

Rating

1.) I am a good and worthwhile person. _____

2.) I am as valuable a person as anyone else. _____

3.) I have good values that guide me in my life. _____

4.) When I look at my eyes in the mirror, I feel good about myself. _____

5.) I feel like I have done well in my life. _____

6.) I can laugh at myself. _____

7.) I like being me. _____

8.) I like myself, even when others reject me. _____

9.) Overall, I am pleased with how I am developing as a person. _____

10.) I love and support myself, regardless of what happens. _____

11.) I would rather be me than someone else. _____

12.) I respect myself. _____

13.) I continue to grow personally. _____

14.) I feel confident about my abilities. _____

15.) I have pride in who I am and what I do. _____

16.) I am comfortable in expressing my thoughts and feelings. _____

17.) I like my body. _____

18.) I handle difficult situations well. _____

19.) Overall, I make good decisions. _____

20.) I am a good friend and people like to be with me. _____

Your total score:

_____

0   100
Total lack of self-esteem   High self-esteem

2

Self-Esteem

Questions to Consider

- What motivated you to enroll in a workshop or seek information regarding building self-esteem?

- What are you hoping to learn?

- What are your personal goals for improving self-esteem?

- Are there particular areas where you feel you lack self-esteem?

- How do you define self-esteem and where do you think it comes from?

- What affects self-esteem?

- Can you think of examples of self-esteem, or lack of self-esteem, in yourself or others?

Self-Esteem

Defining Self-Esteem

Self-esteem is basically the mental image we have of ourselves. Per Merriam-Webster's Collegiate® Dictionary, the word *esteem* as a noun means "worth, value; opinion, judgment; the regard in which one is held…" As a verb, it means "to think very highly or favorably of (someone or something); …to set a high value on; regard highly and prize accordingly."[*] Therefore, self-esteem refers to the value you have for yourself.

Self-esteem is something that comes from within and from gaining an internal sense of personal approval and worth. It can be impacted by how we think and feel about our individual experiences and achievements. Additionally, it may be influenced by *our interpretations* of the responses we receive through interpersonal interactions with others. Note that it is our *interpretations* that impact self-esteem rather than the actual responses or actions of others.

Often, people spend a lot of time concerned with how they are perceived by others, and it is often falsely believed that self-esteem is built through the external validation and approval of the people we interact with; however, it is internal rather than external validation that most directly influences self-esteem. Regardless of how well liked a person may be, relying on the approval and admiration of others for self-worth often backfires because it is our *interpretations* of what others think of us that influences how we feel about ourselves. If we do not feel positively about ourselves, it's nearly impossible to believe that others see us favorably, thus our interpretations are often faulty and we stay stuck in a place of low self-esteem.

It is helpful to view self-esteem as being on a continuum, with low self-esteem on one end and high self-esteem on the other. I tend to use the words negative, low, and unhealthy self-esteem, or positive, high, and healthy self-esteem, interchangeably. People with healthy self-esteem generally have an easier time coping and maintaining self-respect when faced with life's stressors than those who have low self-esteem. When self-esteem is low, it is generally because a person feels unworthy or not good enough. Building self-esteem involves comprehending that, as humans, we all have inherent worth. Recognizing and believing in our inherent worth is an important first step in establishing the groundwork for healthy self-esteem.

---

[*] By permission From *Merriam-Webster's Collegiate® Dictionary, 11th Edition* © 2014 by Merriam-Webster, Inc. (www.Merriam-Webster.com).

Characteristics of Self-Esteem

In *Therapist's Guide to Clinical Intervention: The 1-2-3's of Treatment Planning* (2nd edition), Sharon Johnson lists the following characteristics of low versus high self-esteem:

Characteristics of Low Self-Esteem[*]

- Fearful of exploring his/her real self
- Believes that others are responsible for how he/she feels
- Fearful of taking responsibility for his/her own emotions and actions
- Fearful of assertively communicating wants and needs to others
- Feels and acts like a victim
- Judgmental of self and others
- Does not live according to his/her values (chameleon)
- Covert, phony, "social personality"
- Exaggerates, pretends, lies
- Puts self down, shameful, blaming, self-critical, condemning
- Nice person, approval seeking people pleaser, puts the needs of others first
- Negative attitude
- Triangulates by talking badly about one person to another
- Rationalizes
- Jealous/envious of others, has trouble being genuinely happy for the successes of others
- Perfectionistic
- Dependent/addiction, compulsive, self-defeating thinking and behavior
- Complacent, stagnates, procrastinates
- Does not like the work one does
- Focuses on what doesn't get done instead of what does
- Leaves tasks and relationships unfinished and walks away without resolving issues
- Judges self-worth by comparing to others, feels inferior
- Does not accept or give compliments
- Excessive worry or catastrophizing
- Is not comfortable with self, hard to be alone with self
- Avoids new endeavors, fears mistakes or failure
- Irrational responses, ruled by emotions
- Lack of purpose in life
- Lack of defined goals

---

[*] Copyright © 2004 by Sharon L. Johnson, from *Therapist's Guide to Clinical Intervention: The 1-2-3's of Treatment Planning* (2nd ed.). San Diego, CA: Academic Press, an imprint of Elsevier. Reprinted by permission of Elsevier.

- Feels inadequate to handle new situation, easily stressed
- Feels resentful when doesn't win
- Vulnerable to the opinions, comments, and attitudes of others
- Feels like one's life is in the shadow of another
- Gossips to elevate self
- Continues to blame past experiences (or family) instead of dealing with the current self (the past is an explanation, not an excuse)

Characteristics of High Self-Esteem[*]

- Lives authentically
- Demonstrates self-responsibility—does not blame others
- Takes responsibility for life and consequences of actions
- Sets goals and is committed
- Has purpose in life
- Is emotionally and intellectually honest with self and others
- Confronts and deals with fears
- Is aware of both strengths and weaknesses (self-objective)
- Is self-respected and sets appropriate limits and boundaries
- Does not lie about choices he/she makes
- Self-accepting and self-soothing (does not seek external sources to "make it okay")
- Self-sufficient (thinks and makes decisions independently)
- Does not hold grudges
- Is persistent in all efforts
- Is genuinely grateful
- Positive attitude (cup is half full not half empty)
- Accepts others
- Genuinely pleased for the success of others
- Does not compare oneself to others
- Directs efforts toward being the best he/she can be (recognizes that life is about continual personal growth with an aim for excellence not perfection)
- Lives according to one's own internal values, principles, and standards
- Chooses to see opportunity and challenges instead of problems
- Is spontaneous and enthusiastic about life
- Is able to praise oneself and others for efforts and accomplishments
- Is able to see the big picture versus being trapped by stumbling blocks (mistakes have value)
- Appropriately asks for help and utilizes resources
- Is an active participant in life

- Is comfortable with self and can enjoy alone time
- Is true to oneself
- Has quiet self-confidence

Understanding Self-Worth

Because concepts like self-esteem and self-worth are somewhat abstract, I like to use various visual images and analogies to help conceptualize and reinforce the ideas we are talking about. A great tool that I frequently use to demonstrate inherent worth is one recommended by Ed Jacobs in his book *Creative Counseling Techniques: An Illustrated Guide.* When I talk about self-worth, I often show clients a dollar bill to demonstrate that human worth is inherent and unchanged by external factors. Imagine a dollar bill and think about what it is worth. It's worth a dollar. What if I were to crumple it up, throw it on the floor, kick it, spit on it, and stomp on it. What is it worth now? The answer is that it is still worth a dollar. Regardless of the negative experiences the dollar bill has faced, it is still worth the same amount.

The same is true regarding self-worth. Because you are a person, you have inherent value and self-worth. The experiences that happen to you and the opinions others formulate about you do not affect your core worth as a person. Core worth remains unchanged by external factors. However, your interpretations of various experiences and external opinions, along with your own feelings and thoughts regarding yourself, do impact your self-esteem.

One of the first steps in building self-esteem is grasping the idea that, as a human, you have a fundamental sense of worth. In *The Self-Esteem Workbook,* Glenn R. Schiraldi, Ph.D., talks about the idea of inherent self-worth. He describes five axioms, which he calls Howard's Laws, based on the work of Claudia A. Howard (1992). The axioms are listed below.

Howard's Laws of Human Worth[*]

1. All have infinite, internal, eternal, and unconditional worth as persons.

2. All have equal worth as people. Worth is not comparative or competitive. Although you might be better at sports, academics, or business, and I might be better in social skills, we both have equal worth as human beings.

---

[*] Copyright © 2001. *The Self-Esteem Workbook* by Schiraldi, Glenn R. Reproduced with permission of New Harbinger Publications in the format Republish in a Book via Copyright Clearance Center. Based on the work of Claudia A. Howard.

3. Externals neither add to nor diminish worth. Externals include things like money, looks, performance, and achievements. These only increase one's market or social worth. Worth as a person, however, is infinite and unchanging.

4. Worth is stable and never in jeopardy (even if someone rejects you).

5. Worth doesn't have to be earned or proved. It already exists. Just recognize, accept, and appreciate it.

If your self-esteem is low, it may be difficult to consider that you have inherent self-worth. You may have an easier time accepting and acknowledging the intrinsic worth of others, yet may find it hard to believe the same is true for you. When self-esteem is low, you tend to measure yourself with different standards or with a different ruler than you do the rest of the world. Part of building self-esteem involves beginning to even out the playing field and start judging yourself more fairly. In the following sections, we will explore how irrational thinking sets the stage for this type of unbalanced view and how you can work to offset the damage done to self-esteem.

Self-Esteem is Not Consistent

Self-esteem is not static. Rather, it is something that can change and move in either direction on the continuum over time and with various experiences. Self-esteem is also not consistent across all situations and settings. A person can experience varying levels of self-esteem among different groups of people and within different settings or roles. For example, someone may feel good about herself, confident, and have healthy self-esteem when around friends and family, yet may feel incompetent and experience low self-esteem in the work environment. Or vice versa.

The goal is to achieve healthy, positive self-esteem across all situations within your life. Healthy self-esteem means accepting and being comfortable with yourself as you are—accepting both your strengths and weaknesses. You can still have goals and strive to improve what you see as deficiencies in yourself; however, you don't beat yourself up for having weaknesses or for not being perfect. Healthy self-esteem also involves respecting yourself and maintaining good boundaries with others.

For many people, achieving positive self-esteem often takes time and effort. Maintaining healthy self-esteem is a lifelong, ongoing process that involves growth and change and requires regular attention. The following sections will help you learn tools and strategies to build and maintain self-esteem.

Self-Esteem vs. Self-Confidence

People often confuse the concept of self-esteem with that of self-confidence. Your self-esteem is related to your sense of personal worth and level of self-acceptance, and it can be affected by the degree to which you have self-confidence; however, these concepts are not the same thing. Self-confidence refers to the faith you have in your various abilities, while self-esteem refers to the overall value you have for yourself, given both your strengths and weaknesses.

In *Ten Days to Self-Esteem,* Dr. David Burns provides a useful example using a game of tennis to illustrate the difference between self-esteem and self-confidence. He explains that if a novice tennis player were to play tennis against a professional tennis star, he would likely not have much confidence in his ability to win; however, his self-esteem would remain intact if he were able to rationally understand that losing does not mean he is a bad person or a failure. Losing simply means he's not as skilled at the sport. Therefore, we can lack confidence in certain areas while still recognizing we are worthy and maintaining healthy self-esteem. When self-esteem is low, however, it often causes a person to experience an overall lack of confidence across many areas.

Self-Esteem vs. Arrogance

Some people also worry that building self-esteem will lead to arrogance. They worry that feeling good about themselves will make them appear cocky, arrogant, selfish, or self-centered. When positive feelings about your identity or abilities go to your head, they can cross a line and open you up to the potential to become arrogant or narcissistic. Arrogance happens when you begin taking advantage of or disrespecting others. With healthy self-esteem, you like and respect yourself, but you do so while also respecting others.

The goal of building self-esteem is to recognize and appreciate your sense of personal worth and to value yourself in a way that allows you to live an authentic, happy, and fulfilling life. While doing this, it is important to also respect the values, rights, feelings, and opinions of others. Keeping a healthy balance between respect for yourself and respect for others allows you to maintain a healthy level of self-esteem without crossing a line in terms of becoming arrogant, rude, or conceited.

Nathaniel Branden's Six Pillars of Self-Esteem[*]

In his book *The Six Pillars of Self-Esteem,* Nathaniel Branden outlines six action-based practices he believes form the foundation of self-esteem. They are as follows:

1. Live Consciously:

Living consciously means being aware and mindful of reality in all areas of life. To be aware of your actions, purposes, values, motivations, thoughts, emotions, and sensations. To be present and cognizant of what is going on in each moment and to seek a deeper sense of self-awareness and self-understanding.

2. Self-Acceptance:

"Self-esteem is something we *experience*, while self-acceptance is something we *do*." Self-acceptance means choosing to value yourself and accepting both your strengths and weaknesses. Acceptance doesn't mean liking, enjoying, or condoning everything. It simply means acknowledging and being aware of all parts of who you are. Self-acceptance involves having self-compassion, treating yourself with respect, and being a good friend to yourself.

3. Self-Responsibility:

Self-responsibility means maintaining a sense of personal control over your life and recognizing that you are in charge of and responsible for your choices, actions, decisions, and well-being.

4. Self-Assertiveness:

Self-assertiveness involves being true to yourself and respecting your own thoughts, feelings, beliefs, needs, and wants. It involves a willingness to stand up for yourself and be who you authentically are without putting on a front.

---

[*] Six practices from *The Six Pillars of Self-Esteem* by Nathaniel Branden. Copyright © 1994 by Nathaniel Branden. Used by permission of Bantam Books, an imprint of Random house, a division of Random House LLC. All rights reserved.

5. Live Purposefully:

Living purposefully means being in control of your life. It involves being conscious of your goals and purpose, and demonstrating intention, balance, and self-discipline in your plan of action.

6. Personal Integrity:

Personal integrity involves the integration of ideals, convictions, standards, and beliefs, and matching these things with behavior. It is about being honest, reliable, and trustworthy and ensuring that your words and behaviors are congruent.

These six principles will be helpful to keep in mind as you work to build self-esteem. For a more in-depth look at each principle, please see *The Six Pillars of Self-Esteem* by Nathaniel Branden.

Recommended Journaling

Self-Esteem

I recommend that you begin a self-esteem journal so you will have a special and consistent place to complete homework assignments and further explore the topics discussed in this guide. It is up to you to decide how much or how little you want to engage in the journaling. Many people find doing the suggested journaling very helpful, and those who take the time to use their journal seem to get the most out of the self-esteem-building program. There is something about getting your thoughts and experiences out of your head and onto paper that helps you to work things out and process emotions.

The act of writing can be very cathartic. Often, you will find yourself pouring out thoughts and feelings you didn't even know existed in your head. Your journal is just for you. You can organize and complete it in whatever way you want. Some people like to handwrite on paper, while others prefer to type in a Word document on the computer. There are even online, password-protected diaries you can utilize. You can be artistic and draw or create collages in your journal.

To help encourage journaling and processing questions related to the topic discussed in this workbook, I have created *Building Self-Esteem: A Guide to Achieving Self-Acceptance & a Healthier, Happier Life – Journal Companion.* You may wish to use this journal or you may choose to journal another way. Do whatever helps you to process your thoughts and explore the various topics that are addressed as they relate to your own personal experience.

∞

Self-Esteem—Where you are now:

In your journal, write about anything related to your own self-esteem—thoughts, feelings, experiences. Where on the continuum do you think your self-esteem currently is, overall? Are there situations or roles where you feel your self-esteem is especially high or low? What experiences or which people impact your self-esteem, and in what ways? What do you hope to change about your self-esteem?

Self-Concept Inventory:

In your journal, complete a Self-Concept Inventory, as per the instructions and example that follow. The Self-Concept Inventory can help you to gauge how you currently feel about various aspects of yourself. Save your Self-Concept Inventory, as we will refer back to it in a future chapter.

Self-Concept Inventory[*]

In *Self-Esteem* (3rd edition), Matthew McKay, Ph.D., and Patrick Fanning offer the following exercise, which can help you to get a baseline overview of how you currently feel about yourself in various areas. Also provided is their example for "Eleanor."

Write down as many words or phrases as you can to describe yourself in the following areas:

1. **Physical appearance:** Include descriptions of your height, weight, facial appearance, quality of skin, hair, style of dress, as well as descriptions of specific body areas such as your neck, chest, waist, and legs.

2. **How you relate to others:** Include descriptions of your strengths and weaknesses in intimate relationships and in relationships to friends, family, and co-workers, as well as how you relate to strangers in social settings.

3. **Personality:** Describe your positive and negative personality traits.

4. **How other people see you:** Describe the strengths and weaknesses that your friends and family see.

5. **Performance at school or on the job:** Include descriptions of the way you handle the major tasks at school or work.

6. **Performance of the daily tasks of life:** Descriptions could be included in such areas as hygiene, health, maintenance of your living environment, food preparation, caring for your children, and any other ways you take care of personal or family needs.

---

7. **Mental functioning:** Include here an assessment of how well you reason and solve problems, your capacity for learning and creativity, your general fund of knowledge, your areas of special knowledge, wisdom you have acquired, insight, and so on.

8. **Sexuality:** How you see and feel about yourself as a sexual person.

When you are finished with the inventory, go back and put a plus (+) by items that represent strengths or things that you like about yourself. Put a minus (-) by items that you consider weaknesses or would like to change about yourself. Don't mark items that are neutral, factual observations about yourself.

Example Self-Concept Inventory[*]

Eleanor, a sales representative for a pharmaceutical company, completed her Self-Concept Inventory as follows:

1. Physical Appearance

    + Large brown eyes   - Flat chested
    + Dark curly hair   - Ugly nose
    + Olive complexion   - Look good in '30s-style dresses
    + Clear, young-looking skin   + Don't need makeup
    - Buckteeth   Like jeans and T-shirts
    - Fat belly   Long neck
    - Fat thighs   5 feet 5 inches
    + Well-shaped hips   130 lbs

2. How I Relate to Others

    + Warm   + Socially competent
    + Open   + Good listener
    + Accepting & flexible   - Can't ask for what I want
    - Can't set limits or say no   - Uncomfortable with strangers
    - Too accepting, then resentful   + Protective
    + Good communicator   + Good at compromises
    + Entertaining   - Use guilt to get kids to do things
    - Phony with friends   - Sometimes attack/nag the kids

3. Personality

    + Responsible   - Blabbermouth
    + Funny   - Sulky when I don't get my way
    + Open and outgoing   - Sometimes irritable
    + Friendly   - Try too hard to please
    - Hate being alone   + Affectionate with family
    + Love to be busy

4. How others see me

    - Wishy-washy   + Funny
    - Overextended   + Strong

- Forgetful
- Lose everything
+ Positive
+ Competent

+ Independent
+ Warm
- Scattered
- Know-nothing

5. Performance on the job

+ Prompt
+ Hardworking, motivated
+ Likable
+ Put people at ease
- Overstressed
- Restless

- Lousy on the phone
- Avoid making sales calls
+ Knowledgeable in the field
+ Good at selling
- Screw up paperwork

6. Performance of daily tasks of life

- Forget appointments
- Put things off
+ Good hygiene
+ Quick, competent cook
- Lousy housekeeper

+ Conscientious about teeth
+ Conscientious with baby's safety
+ Conscientious with cleanliness
- Shop stupidly
+ Don't fret about my appearance

7. Mental functioning

- Lousy at arguing, debating
- Stupid about current events
- Mentally lazy
+ Intuitive
- Illogical

+ Like to learn new things
+ Curious
+ Quick mind
- Uncreative

8. Sexuality

+ Usually turned on, interested
+ Accepting of partner's sexual turn-ons
- Inhibited
- Afraid to initiate

+ Communicate sexual preferences well
+ Can express feelings sexually
- Can feel very rejected and depressed
- Passive

3

Self-Talk

Questions to Consider

- How often are you aware of the internal messages or thoughts going on inside your head?

- Do you pay attention to the types of thoughts you think about yourself? If so, what do they tend to be like?

- Do you find it difficult to be kind to yourself and to give yourself praise? Can you think of any positive messages you have told yourself recently?

- Do you frequently berate yourself for shortcomings, weaknesses, and failures? If so, what sort of messages do you tend to say? Can you think of recent examples?

- Are you aware of any belief systems or personal values that get in the way of happiness, success, or feeling good about yourself?

- Have you ever told yourself you are not capable before giving yourself the chance to try?

Self-Talk

Self-talk refers to the silent messages or internal thoughts we think all day long. It is something everybody does and is not the same as "hearing voices," which is symptomatic of hallucinations or serious disorders, such as schizophrenia. Self-talk comes from that little voice, or the internal monologue, in the back of each of our heads that constantly gives us messages, makes interpretations, and thinks numerous thoughts as we go about our various tasks throughout the day. Sometimes these messages seem very loud and clear, while other times they are very subtle, and we often do not even realize we are thinking anything at all. But we are always thinking and essentially talking to ourselves inside our heads. This self-talk voice is very powerful and plays a large role in how you feel.

Positive/Healthy Self-Talk Versus Negative/Unhealthy Self-Talk

When your self-talk is positive and upbeat, you generally feel good. However, positive self-talk does not always come naturally. Instead, self-talk that is largely negative seems to be the norm for many people. This is especially true for those with depression, anxiety, or low self-esteem. Often, people with these conditions have unknowingly developed a pattern and habit of constantly engaging in negative self-talk and dysfunctional thinking.

Negative feelings, such as frustration, anger, depression, guilt, hopelessness, and fear are often caused by negative self-talk. The idea behind self-talk is that your *thoughts,* not actual events or things, create your moods and the way you feel about yourself and various experiences. In other words, the bad things that happen do not really cause us to become upset. We get upset because of the way we *think* about and interpret these events. When we feel upset about something, it is ultimately the thought "I feel bad" or "I don't like this" that creates the feeling. We do not readily recognize the actual thoughts behind events or objects because, often, they are subconscious and we are not used to paying close attention to this internal chatter.

An Example

I once backed out of a driveway and smacked right into another parked car. I immediately felt upset and terrible about myself. Since I was aware of the concept of self-talk and had become pretty good at catching destructive thinking, I was able to stop and recognize the messages going through the back of my head and realize these thoughts were not helping the situation. The thoughts included sentences like, "You idiot. You are so stupid. You should have looked in your mirror. This is terrible. Fixing the dent is going to cost a fortune. How could you be so careless? Now you are going to have to tell the car owner what happened, and she will hate you." I felt awful. However, the bad feelings were not actually coming from the act of me hitting another car. They were coming from the fact that I was beating myself up for it and engaging in a lot of negative thinking. Because I was in the habit of catching destructive thoughts, I was able to recognize and stop the negative messages and instead tell myself, "Okay, this stinks. But it's not the end of the world. Everybody makes mistakes and you are going to be okay." I immediately felt my mood lift and, by ending the self-depreciating messages, I was able to protect my self-esteem.

Negative Self-Talk & Low Self-Esteem

Your internal monologue frequently involves thoughts specifically related to who you are and how you feel about yourself. When self-esteem is low, we wind up constantly sending ourselves messages about our inadequacies and our faults, and we focus on the negative experiences we face. These negative thoughts include sentences that are self-rejecting and self-depreciating, which further deplete self-esteem and cause feelings of depression. Negative self-talk and low self-esteem become a vicious cycle. The worse we feel about ourselves, the more we beat ourselves up with our thinking. And the more negative thoughts we have about ourselves, the lower our self-esteem becomes.

Everybody experiences negative self-talk to some extent. For some people, negative self-talk becomes so pervasive that it becomes impossible to feel happy or good enough. When negative self-talk is at its worst, a person may seek out various coping mechanisms to help alleviate the bad feelings and essentially block out the negative voice. These coping mechanisms can often be unhealthy or even dangerous. They can include things like excessive use of drugs and alcohol, promiscuity, self-injurious behaviors, such as cutting, or sometimes even suicide attempts. Negative self-talk is essentially a bad habit that can lead to devastating consequences, but the good news is that self-talk is something we can change. The first step involves gaining a better understanding of how negative self-talk shows up in our thinking.

Dysfunctional Thinking

Two counseling theories that involve identifying faulty thinking include Rational Emotive Behavior Therapy (REBT) and Cognitive Behavioral Therapy (CBT). These theories emphasize a focus on identifying, challenging, and replacing negative self-talk and dysfunctional patterns of thinking with healthier thoughts to create growth and change. They encompass the idea that faulty thinking creates negative emotions and exacerbates problems.

REBT is an action-based form of psychotherapy initially developed by Albert Ellis in the 1950s. Ellis believed that emotional disturbances were caused by flawed or irrational thinking. He taught that people are disturbed by their view of things, rather than by actual events, and he helped patients to manage their emotions and behaviors by identifying and altering irrational thinking.

Similar to REBT, CBT is another goal-oriented form of psychotherapy that looks at changing thought patterns to treat a wide range of issues. In the 1970s, Aaron Beck laid much of the groundwork for CBT and began identifying various forms of cognitive distortions. In the 1980s, his student David Burns popularized these concepts via his book *Feeling Good: The New Mood Therapy.* Like REBT, CBT focuses on looking at and changing dysfunctional thought patterns. Beck and Burns are credited with researching and categorizing what are referred to as "cognitive distortions" or "self-defeating beliefs," essentially attitudes that control our way of thinking and make us vulnerable to low self-esteem, negative emotions, and conflicts in relationships.

Irrational beliefs and cognitive distortions are often rigid, harsh, and very unrealistic. They set us up to feel disappointed or inadequate because they do not leave room for flexibility or other options. Engaging in thinking that is filled with self-defeating beliefs will keep you trapped in a place of low self-esteem and make it nearly impossible to feel happy, confident, and fulfilled. For an in-depth look at cognitive distortions and strategies to untwist your negative thinking, see *Ten Days to Self-Esteem* by David Burns. Below we will explore some of the common patterns of dysfunctional thinking as they relate specifically to thoughts regarding self-esteem and self-worth.

Irrational Beliefs

Albert Ellis listed the following examples of common irrational beliefs that frequently begin in childhood and wind up causing problems later in adulthood if they remain part of our core belief systems:

Common Irrational Beliefs of Children

- I must be liked by everyone, and if I am not it is awful and I can't stand it.

- If someone calls me names, it must be true and I can't stand it.

- I should be the best at everything I do and if I'm not, I am worthless.

- Some people are bad and I have to dwell on how to get back at them.

- It is awful when things are not the way I would very much like them to be.

- My unhappiness is caused by others and I have no ability to control my unhappiness and have no ability to make myself happy.

- It is easier for me to avoid certain troubling situations than to face them.

- I cannot depend on myself—I have to depend on others for my strength.

- My past causes me to be the way I am and there is nothing I can do about it.

- There is a perfect solution to every problem and it is terrible if I cannot figure out the perfect solution.

- I must become upset and stay upset over other people's problems.

- Things should be fair, and if they are not it is awful and I can't stand it.

- I should never be uncomfortable or inconvenienced and when I am it is awful and I can't stand it.

- I can achieve and be successful even if I do nothing and have no plan of action.

- It is my fault if my parents fight (drink, are getting divorced).

- Because I am adopted (in foster care, have less money), I am less than other kids are.

- Because he/she did that to me (mean action; physical, sexual, emotional abuse), there is something wrong with me and I don't deserve to be happy.

- If I love my stepdad (stepmom), it means I don't love my dad (mom).

These irrational beliefs often begin in childhood but continue on into adulthood to form the basis of the messages incorporated into people's negative self-talk and dysfunctional thought patterns. Irrational beliefs may not show up as actual sentences you say out loud or establish in a concrete form. Instead, they are subconscious beliefs or attitudes that you hold somewhere in the back of your mind. When you do or experience something that goes against one of these self-defeating beliefs, you are unable to justify or make sense of the experience. Thus, you wind up feeling upset, disappointed, or somehow inadequate.

As you become more aware of your own feelings and self-talk, you will be better able to recognize various forms of dysfunctional thinking and can work to change irrational thoughts into statements that are more supportive of a healthy and rational outlook on life. Consider the first example: "I must be liked by everyone, and if I am not it is awful and I can't stand it." Yes, it would be nice to always be liked by everyone. But let's face it: That just is not realistic. There are always going to be people who, for whatever reason, may not like you. If you hold on to a belief that makes being disliked unbearable, you will inevitably face feelings of frustration and inadequacy at some point or another.

Another example of an irrational belief that many people hold is that it is wrong to feel or show negative emotions. Some people grow up in families where they receive the message that showing emotions is weak or unacceptable; thus, they feel guilty and inadequate when experiencing various emotions. This view that emotions are off-limits is faulty because it is irrational to expect that you will never experience or display negative emotions. Everyone encounters situations and experiences that are out of our control, which can lead to feelings of sadness, anger, fear, or being overwhelmed. Sometimes we simply are unable to control or hide these emotions in the moment. By telling yourself that you should never experience or show negative emotions, you basically set yourself up for failure because that is just not possible. Experiencing emotions is not a choice, but what we do with them or how we express them is.

If you can learn to instead incorporate more rational, realistic thoughts into your belief system, such as "Even though I am a good person, there are bound to be some people who don't like me for reasons out of my control" and "Experiencing a range of emotions is a normal part of life," then you become less hard on yourself. You leave room for the inevitable times when things will be less than perfect or ideal. By thinking more rationally, you cut yourself some slack and avoid the pitfall of beating yourself up with destructive negative self-talk messages that imply you are a failure or a terrible person if you are not liked or if you get angry.

In *Feeling Better, Getting Better, Staying Better: Profound Self-Help Therapy for Your Emotions,* Albert Ellis says that irrational beliefs fall under the following three categories:

- I *absolutely must* perform well!
- I *absolutely must* be treated fairly by others!
- I *must not* find life's conditions very hard![*]

These rigid beliefs do not leave room for error or other options, thus they set the stage for a letdown. Because they are unrealistic and not entirely possible, they tend to lead to failure, frustration, and disappointment. Since the beliefs are about personal standards, the inability to meet them negatively impacts feelings of self-worth and lowers self-esteem.

Distorted Thinking

Below are examples of common forms of dysfunctional thinking. Like irrational beliefs, these ways of thinking often become habitual patterns that are very engrained in people's subconscious thinking. Nearly everyone has engaged in distorted thinking in one way or another. When dysfunctional thinking becomes a habit or norm in thinking, it can be very difficult to recognize the distortions, yet they have a tremendous impact on how we feel and approach various endeavors. When your thinking includes irrational beliefs and dysfunctional distortions, you become prone to negative self-talk and problems like low self-esteem, depression, and anxiety.

Black-and-white, all-or-nothing, or **polarized thinking** occurs when you look at things in black-or-white terms. In regard to self-esteem, when you engage in this type of thinking you tend to evaluate your personal qualities in extremes. When you make a mistake or do not do as well as you wanted, you see yourself as being totally worthless, terrible, a loser, etc. You may think that the only way to be a worthwhile person is to do things perfectly. This is distorted thinking because no one is all bad or all good and it is impossible to be perfect all the time. Everyone has both good qualities and flaws and weaknesses. Examples of all-or-nothing thinking include sentences like, "I fail at everything I do," "I don't enjoy anything," "I am completely incompetent," or "Nothing ever works out for me." Words that convey extremes, such as *always, never, every, all,* and *none,* are used.

Magnification, also called **catastrophizing,** is frequently used by people with low self-esteem. Every mistake, failure, or perceived problem tends to be blown out of proportion and dwelled upon for long periods of time. It becomes difficult to cut yourself slack or forgive yourself for even very minor things. For example, you may beat yourself up for something you thought you did wrong or something stupid you thought you said, thus making yourself feel even worse and further depleting your self-esteem. You may also overemphasize the importance of an event; for example, you may think something like, "Since I didn't do so well on that project, this must be the wrong field for me. Maybe I should give up."

Minimization is the opposite of magnification and occurs when you underemphasize or devalue something positive that happens. For example, if somebody does something nice for you, you assume they are just doing it because they feel they have to, not because they really care about you or believe you are worthy. When you do have successes, you downplay their importance. You may tell yourself something like, "Yeah, I may have won second place, but I didn't come in first."

Tunnel vision or **overgeneralization** happens when you see only what fits in your frame of mind and ignore the rest. If you make a mistake or have trouble doing something as well as you would like, you then predict that you will *never* be able to do well and will *always* make the same mistake. Examples would be, "Because I didn't make the varsity team, I should just give up playing soccer. I'll never be good enough," or "Since I failed this time, I should just give up completely because I will never do it right."

Negative focus, sometimes also referred to as **negative mental filter** or **dwelling on the negatives,** happens when you concentrate on mistakes, things that did not go well, or negative aspects of yourself, while failing to recognize positive aspects and accomplishments. You tend to magnify negative things and minimize positives about yourself. For example, you think, "I only got a 75 percent on the test. I am terrible at math." You ignore the fact that you may have tried your best and that, even though you did not get a perfect score, you still got more answers right than wrong.

Discounting or rejecting the positives happens when you *ignore* positive qualities in yourself altogether or dismiss them completely. When someone says something good about you, you overlook or deflect the compliment. You may often find yourself saying "Yeah, but..." For example, "Yeah, I did well, but that was only because it was easy," or "It doesn't count that I did well because anyone could do that."

Assuming, jumping to conclusions, or **arbitrary inference** occurs when a person makes an unfounded judgment or assumes the worst as his/her default. It often shows up in **mind reading,** when you assume others disapprove of or negatively judge you without valid reason. This is often based on a negative view of yourself and your irrational interpretations, rather that on what others are actually thinking. For example, if you feel bad about yourself you may assume things like, "He thinks I'm a loser" or "She doesn't like me." Jumping to conclusions and discounting the positives sometimes occurs at the same time as when you deflect compliments. For example, "He told me I look nice but he probably just said that to get me on his good side."

Predicting the future is another form of jumping to conclusions that is based in always assuming the worst. Somebody who engages in this form of distorted thinking tends to have a pessimistic, "glass-half-empty" view of the world or of himself/herself. When this negative view is internalized and pointed toward oneself, it is impossible to have healthy self-esteem because self-confidence is constantly destroyed. Part of the danger in engaging in this type of thinking is that it can end up creating self-fulfilling prophecies. For example, if you go into a situation thinking, "I will fail," chances are you will not do as well as if you had given yourself an optimistic pep talk and instead said something like, "I will do just fine" or "I am going to try my best."

Subjective reasoning or **emotional reasoning** happens when you make feelings facts. You believe your own negative feelings in a situation are proof that you are inadequate. For example, if you feel like a loser in a given instance, you assume it must be a fact that you are a loser in general.

Name-calling or **labeling** is something people do when they haphazardly call themselves names like "stupid" or "dummy." Remember my own personal example of backing into another car: My immediate thought was, "You idiot." When you give yourself a negative label or call yourself a mean name, you are disrespecting yourself and, thus, reinforcing low self-esteem.

Personalization or **blame** happens when you assume too much responsibility for a negative event. You incorrectly decide that what happened was your fault or reflects your inadequacy, even when there is no basis for doing so. You fail to see others as capable of flaws or personal deficits and instead believe any issues or conflicts must be your fault. If you actually do hold some responsibility, you magnify your role in the conflict and beat yourself up with self-depreciating thoughts.

Should statements include messages that begin with things like, "I should," "I should not," "I must," "I cannot," "I need," etc. These types of messages can be formed either consciously as a directive ("I should go to the store today") or subconsciously as part of your belief system ("I should be perfect"). Should statements are harmful because they are often rigid and unrealistic. They can create feelings of anger, guilt, frustration, and resentment because, realistically, we cannot always meet the strict expectations and criteria that lay behind the "should."

More on Should Statements

Albert Ellis, known for his blunt and controversial language, referred to the act of fixating on maladaptive sentences that begin with words like *should, ought, must,* and *have to* as "musterbation" and warned his patients not to "should all over themselves." He demonstrated how thinking in ways that include absolutes and demands set us up for frustration, failure, and disappointment.

Examples of common should statements include sentences like:

- I should be more patient and kind.
- I must not put my own needs first.
- I have to keep the peace.
- I need to protect other people's feelings.
- I should never make mistakes.
- I must be respectful of others even when they don't respect me.
- I have to be perfect.
- I need to accomplish x, y, and z.
- I should not rock the boat.

The problem with these statements is that they are too strict and inflexible. They do not leave room for mistakes or imperfections, which are part of life. Changing should statements into less rigid sentences can ultimately help to prevent or decrease negative feelings, such as disappointment and frustration, and can help protect self-esteem by avoiding the pitfall that is inevitable when you continuously set yourself up for failure. By simply using slightly different language, you allow for more flexibility and establish standards and expectations that are less severe and more reasonable. Changing just one or two words can have a huge effect in terms of creating conditions that are more realistic, forgiving, and protective of self-esteem.

Examples of should substitutes:
- I should..............................I could
- I must................................I'd like to
- I have to.............................I choose to
- I need to.............................I want to

For example, the statement or thought, "I should do all my chores today" is very rigid and too likely to become problematic. If you listed ALL of the chores you hope to accomplish and tell yourself you *should* do them all, you may feel very overwhelmed at the thought of having to do so much. Additionally, you may experience a sense of resistance regarding feeling obligated. This statement creates anxiety up front and does not leave room for things to go wrong. It sets you up to feel discouraged, frustrated, and angry with yourself if you are unable to do everything you had planned.

Self-talk that includes "should" statements puts you at risk for more self-talk that contains "I failed" messages later. When you do not accomplish something behind a "should," that negative self-talk creeps in, responding to the should statement by saying things like, "You didn't do what you were supposed to. You are a failure. You are irresponsible. You can't manage your time well." It is highly likely that something may come up that takes time out of your day and you might not get everything on your to-do list accomplished. Regardless of the reason, if you are unable to accomplish everything after telling yourself, "I should," you will inevitably feel bad and likely will be upset with yourself in the end.

You wind up feeling bad about *yourself* for not accomplishing what you had told yourself you *should* do. The focus shifts from being about the list of chores to instead being about how you are a failure. This is bad for your mood and ultimately for your self-esteem.

By changing this should statement up front to something less rigid, such as, "I would like to get all of my chores done today," you allow yourself more flexibility. If you do not get to everything, you may still feel disappointed, but you do not feel bad about *yourself* for not accomplishing everything. Instead of beating yourself up, your self-talk will likely be more rational, saying things such as, "I wish I got more things accomplished today." This type of self-talk is not berating or belittling, thus you protect yourself from damaged self-esteem and overwhelmingly negative feelings.

Mistaken Beliefs

In *The Anxiety & Phobia Workbook* (4th edition), Dr. Edmund J. Bourne uses the terminology *mistaken beliefs* to encompass the problematic beliefs and assumptions we make about ourselves, others, and life in general. He provides the following questionnaire to help individuals identify the types of faulty thinking they engage in. Fill out the following questions to help gauge whether you hold any mistaken beliefs in your personal belief system.

Mistaken Beliefs Questionnaire[*]

How much does each of these unconstructive beliefs influence your feelings and behavior? Take your time to reflect about each belief.

> 1 = Not so much
> 2 = Somewhat / sometimes
> 3 = Strongly / frequently
> 4 = Very strongly

Place the appropriate number after each statement.

1.) I feel powerless or helpless. _____
2.) Often I feel like a victim of outside circumstances. _____
3.) I don't have the money to do what I really want. _____
4.) There is seldom enough time to do what I want. _____
5.) Life is very difficult—It's a struggle. _____
6.) If things are going well, watch out! _____
7.) I feel unworthy. I feel that I'm not good enough. _____
8.) Often I feel that I don't deserve to be happy or successful. _____
9.) Often I feel a sense of defeat and resignation: "Why bother?" _____
10.) My condition seems hopeless. _____
11.) There is something fundamentally wrong with me. _____
12.) I feel ashamed of my condition. _____
13.) If I take risks to get better, I'm afraid I'll fail. _____

14.) If I take risks to get better, I'm afraid I'll succeed. _____

15.) If I felt better, I might have to deal with realities I'd rather not face. _____

16.) I feel like I'm nothing (or can't make it) unless I'm loved. _____

17.) I can't stand being separated from others. _____

18.) If a person doesn't love me in return, I feel like it's my fault. _____

19.) It's very hard to be alone. _____

20.) What others think of me is very important. _____

21.) I feel personally threatened when criticized. _____

22.) It's important to please others. _____

23.) People won't like me if they see who I really am. _____

24.) I need to keep up a front or others will see my weaknesses. _____

25.) I have to achieve or produce something significant to feel okay about myself. _____

26.) My accomplishments at work/school are extremely important. _____

27.) Success is everything. _____

28.) I have to be the best at what I do. _____

29.) I have to be somebody—somebody outstanding. _____

30.) To fail is terrible. _____

31.) I can't rely on others for help. _____

32.) I can't receive from others. _____

33.) If I let someone get too close, I'm afraid of being controlled. _____

34.) I can't tolerate being out of control. _____

35.) I'm the only one who can solve my problems. _____

36.) I should always be very generous and unselfish. _____

37.) I should always be the perfect:
a. Employee _____
b. Professional _____
c. Spouse _____
d. Parent _____
e. Lover _____
f. Friend _____
g. Student _____
h. Son/Daughter _____

38.) I should be able to endure any hardship. _____

39.) I should be able to find a quick solution to every problem. _____

40.) I should never be tired or fatigued. _____

41.) I should always be efficient. _____

42.) I should always be competent. _____

43.) I should always be able to foresee everything. _____

44.) I should never be angry or irritable. _____

45.) I should always be pleasant or nice no matter how I feel. _____

46.) I often feel:
a. Ugly _____

      b. Inferior or defective   _____

      c. Unintelligent   _____

      d. Guilty or ashamed   _____

47.)   I'm just the way I am—I can't really change.   _____

48.)   The world outside is a dangerous place.   _____

49.)   Unless you worry about a problem it just gets worse.   _____

50.)   It's risky to trust people.   _____

51.)   My problems will go away on their own with time.   _____

52.)   I feel anxious about making mistakes.   _____

53.)   I demand perfection of myself.   _____

54.)   If I didn't have my safe person (or safe place), I'm afraid I couldn't cope.   _____

55.)   If I stop worrying, I'm afraid something bad will happen.   _____

56.)   I'm afraid to face the world out there on my own.   _____

57.)   My self-worth isn't a given—it has to be earned.   _____

Mistaken Beliefs Questionnaire Scoring [*]

You may have noticed that some of the beliefs on the questionnaire fall into specific groups, each of which reflects a very basic belief or attitude toward life. (The idea for defining subgroups of beliefs was adapted from David Burns's work.) Go back over your answers and see how you scored with respect to each of the groups of beliefs listed below.

Add your scores for each of the following subgroups of beliefs. If your total score on the items in a particular subgroup exceeds the criterion value, then this is likely to be a problem area for you. It's important that you give this subgroup special attention when you begin to work with affirmations to start changing your mistaken beliefs.

     1.) _____

     2.) _____

     7.) _____

     9.) _____

   10.) _____

   11.) _____

  TOTAL: _____

If your total score is over 15: You likely believe that you are powerless, have little or no control over outside circumstances, or are unable to do much that could help your situation. In sum, "I'm powerless" or "I can't do much about my life."

---

[*] The idea for defining subgroups of beliefs was adapted form David Burns, M.D., *Feeling Good.* See his book for further details on how to counter and work with mistaken beliefs.

16.) _____
17.) _____
18.) _____
19.) _____
54.) _____
56.) _____

TOTAL: _____

If your total score is over 15: You likely believe that your self-worth is dependent on the love of someone else. You feel that you need another's (or others') love to feel okay about yourself and to cope. In sum, "My worth and security are dependent on being loved."

20.) _____
21.) _____
22.) _____
23.) _____
24.) _____
45.) _____

TOTAL: _____

If your total score is over 15: You likely believe that your self-worth is dependent on others' approval. Being pleasing and getting acceptance from others is very important for your sense of security and your sense of who you are. In sum, "My worth and security depend on the approval of others."

25.) _____
26.) _____
27.) _____
28.) _____
29.) _____
30.) _____
41.) _____
42.) _____

TOTAL: _____

If your total score is over 20: You likely believe that your self-worth is dependent on external achievements, such as school or career performance, status, or wealth. In sum, "My worth is dependent on my performance or achievements."

31.) _____
32.) _____
33.) _____
34.) _____
35.) _____
50.) _____

TOTAL: _____

If your score is over 15: You likely believe that you can't trust, rely on, or receive help from others. You may have a tendency to keep a distance from people and avoid intimacy for fear of losing control. In sum, "If I trust or get too close, I'll lose control."

37.) _____

38.) _____

39.) _____

40.) _____

52.) _____

53.) _____

TOTAL: _____

If your score is over 25: You likely believe that you have to be perfect in some or many areas of life. You make excessive demands on yourself. There is no room for mistakes. In sum, "I have to be perfect" or "It's not okay to make mistakes."

Self-Talk Up Close & Personal

A client of mine was struggling with such bad negative self-talk that it was creating a multitude of problems, including anxiety, depression, self-injury, and suicidal ideation. Using poetry to express her feelings and struggles, she wrote the following poem to explain the thinking that goes on inside her head. I feel very humbled that she shared this vulnerable part of herself with me and I was blown away by what a great job she did in terms of putting her struggles into words.

The poem is sad and intense because it shows how painful her feelings had become; however it provides such a powerful example of how simple yet pervasive and destructive self-talk messages can be. This client is a great person. She is kind, talented, creative, smart, pretty, and an absolute joy to know. It is obvious that her friends and family adore her and that they are loving and supportive. Unfortunately, she developed a pattern of negative self-talk early on and, over time, it has created low self-esteem and the inability to see herself in the positive light others do. She is a perfect example of how struggles with negative self-talk can happen to anyone and can wreak havoc on an otherwise normal, healthy, happy life.

I am very grateful to my client for granting me permission to share her poem. Please note that the poem contains language that some may find inappropriate or offensive. My client and I discussed whether she should change the language before giving a copy to me, however I think it is important to convey how incredibly strong the feelings of frustration and anger can become after years of negative self-talk.

———•———

Buried Alive

I have anxiety.
Now most people think it means I'm crazy or get startled easily.
That is not quite true...
It's more of a crazy that's inside of you.
And for me it's a whirlwind of thoughts in my brain
And if people could hear them they would think I'm insane.
These thoughts shouldn't be here.
I would give anything for my head just to be clear.
At least then I would be free of my messed-up anxiety.
Oh well, that's just how I function.
Having a brain that overanalyzes so my head is a fucked-up junction.
Pointless thoughts spinning around, slowly burying me into the ground.

I'll give you an example so you can see just how fucked-up my brain can be.
I'm walking down the hall and say hi to a person I know,
we then pass each other and continue to go.
A simple interaction you think? Ha-ha...NO.
Most people wouldn't even think twice about it, because it's a meaningless thing,
but my brain seems to doubt it
Here is how my brain works: Should I have said hi instead of hey?
Goddamnit, hi is super gay!
Should I have stopped and talked to them? I doubt I'm even their friend.
They probably think I'm weird as hell!
They probably hate me...but I hate me, too, so oh well.
I'm so fucking stupid, I'm so fucking dumb,
how can I not handle a simple situation.

As you can see my thought patterns escalate quite quickly.
Every interaction I have is like I'm in a grave slowly being buried alive,
by the words that haunt me on the inside.
They're all shovels filled with dirt, slowly burying me with my hurt.
I have no way to escape or survive...All I can do is be buried alive.

———•———

While this poem is dark and conveys deep hurt, I love that it is so real. It demonstrates the agonizing that can go on in somebody's head over something as simple as saying "hi" versus "hey." For people with low self-esteem and negative self-talk, this constant analysis and second-guessing of personal actions makes up the continuous chatter that generates problems and creates barriers to happiness and healthy self-esteem. Realistically, most likely nobody else even notices or gives a second thought to the word choice we use when saying hello, yet our own negative self-talk voice convinces us we are wrong or inadequate. In this poem, you can see how name-calling, mind reading, and making interpretations play out and create self-deprecation and pain.

From the outside looking in, it is easy to see how unnecessary this self-berating is; however when your self-esteem is low and you are stuck in the habit of beating yourself up mentally, it can be incredibly difficult to recognize the problem and make changes. You begin to feel completely unworthy and hold yourself to different standards than you do the rest of the world. You do not feel deserving of self-acceptance or kind words from yourself. Nevertheless, with awareness, effort, determination, and practice, it is possible to shift the way you treat yourself and build self-esteem.

Ending the Habit of Negative Self-Talk

When you learn to recognize negative self-talk and become more aware of your internal thought processes, you can work to change the way you think on a regular basis. By stopping dysfunctional thinking, you can change the overall way you feel. Learning to stop the negative voice is a healthy coping mechanism and a tool we can all benefit from. The ultimate goal is to end the negative messages and instead incorporate healthy, positive self-talk statements into your thinking—a practice that will improve your self-esteem and help you to feel better.

In *Rewire Your Brain: Think Your Way to a Better Life*, John B. Arden, Ph.D., talks about neuroplasticity and describes how the brain is constantly changing and being modified by experiences throughout your life. He says that new brain cells can be born and states, "repetition rewires the brain and breeds habit." Dr. Arden describes a process for rewiring the brain by unlearning old habits and creating new ones using the acronym FEED[*], which stands for Focus, Effort, Effortlessness, and Determination.

Focus involves paying attention to the new behavior you want to learn or the situation you want to change. In regard to self-talk, this means you begin to notice the various messages in your internal dialogue and consider how these messages can be more self-serving rather than self-destructive.

---

[*] Adapted from John B. Arden, Ph.D.'s 2010 *Rewire Your Brain: Think Your Way to a Better Life*. Hoboken, NJ: John Wiley & Sons, Inc. Used with permission.

The **effort** involved in focusing activates your brain to establish new synaptic connections, helping you to learn new things. With practice, which takes **effort**, the new behavior, thought, or feeling becomes established and ultimately takes less energy to keep going. The new behavior eventually becomes **effortless**.

Regarding self-talk, the more and more you practice catching and changing negative self-talk messages, the easier it will become. Eventually, your overall way of thinking and talking to yourself will shift and positive self-talk will become more of the norm.

Determination is essential in putting forth the effort involved in working to change the behavior and keep up with the new way of thinking. Although it takes some hard work and a dedicated effort to focus, practice, and stay determined, you *can* ultimately conquer negative self-talk, rewire the brain, and change your whole outlook on yourself, thus creating a foundation of healthy self-esteem.

It is not always easy to change self-talk because chances are you have been engaging in negative self-talk for a very long time. Most of us know that bad habits are generally hard to break. But with patience and practice, it's possible. Chapter five provides more help on changing negative self-talk messages into rational statements that will ultimately begin forming a new pattern of healthy thinking.

Recommended Journaling

Self-Talk

Complete the Mistaken Beliefs Questionnaire. This will help you to identify areas where you may engage in distorted thinking, which ultimately impacts your sense of self. Which questions do you very strongly agree with? Do you see any pattern among the questions you scored with a four? Are you able to see how these statements involve negative self-talk and irrational beliefs?

Over the course of the next few weeks, begin to pay attention to the voice in the back of your mind and try to figure out what thoughts you are thinking throughout the day. Are you able to identify times when you engage in negative self-talk? It may be helpful to jot some of these thoughts down in your journal. You may begin to see a pattern in your thinking and may be able to identify certain areas that trip you up the most. Pay special attention to your self-talk during times when you feel negative emotions—angry, upset, hurt, frustrated. What thoughts may be behind these emotions? Try to formulate the thoughts into sentences, then work to identify and dispute any irrational thinking.

If you catch yourself engaging in irrational thinking or resonate with any of the irrational beliefs or forms of dysfunctional thinking listed in the examples, consider where these ideas come from. Think about what the pros and cons are of changing these beliefs to include more rational ways of looking at things.

Remember that negative self-talk is often a long-term, deep-seated habit and a familiar pattern of thinking. It will likely be challenging at first to catch your negative self-talk and pinpoint your irrational beliefs. Give yourself credit for the times you are aware that you are engaging in distorted thinking rather than beating yourself up for doing so. With time and practice, it will become easier to identify, and eventually to prevent or alter, toxic thinking.

Perfectionism

Questions to Consider

- Do you tend to give more weight to your accomplishments or to your failures?

- Do you focus more on your strengths or on your weaknesses? Can you list each?

- Are you inclined to set very rigid standards for yourself? Provide examples.

- Do you have a hard time making decisions because you are afraid of making a wrong or bad choice?

- Do you often feel "not good enough"?

Perfectionism

Perfectionist tendencies are often a major driving force behind negative self-talk, irrational thinking, and problems with low self-esteem. Because perfectionism is such a common problem for so many people, it deserves some further exploration.

In *The Gifts of Imperfection: Let Go of Who You Think You're Supposed to Be and Embrace Who You Are*, Brené Brown discusses perfectionism, saying it is "a self-destructive and addictive belief system." Brown says that shame is the birthplace of perfection and describes shame as the painful experience of feeling flawed and therefore believing you are unworthy of love and belonging. She says that perfectionism does not prevent things like judgment or blame. Rather, "Research shows that perfectionism hampers success. In fact, it's often the path to depression, anxiety, addiction, and life-paralysis."[*]

In *Daring Greatly: How the Courage to Be Vulnerable Transforms the Way We Live, Love, Parent, and Lead,* Brené Brown discusses perfectionism further, saying:

- Perfectionism is not the same thing as striving for excellence. Perfectionism is not about healthy achievement and growth. Perfectionism is a defensive move. It's the belief that if we do things perfectly and look perfect, we can minimize or avoid the pain of blame, judgment, and shame. Perfectionism is a twenty-ton shield that we lug around, thinking it will protect us, when I fact it's the thing that's really preventing us from being seen.

- Perfectionism is not self-improvement. Perfectionism is, at its core, about trying to earn approval. Most perfectionists grew up being praised for achievement and performance (grades, manners, rule following, people pleasing, appearance, sports). Somewhere along the way, they adopted this dangerous and debilitating belief system: "I am what I accomplish and how well I accomplish it. Please. Perform. Perfect." Healthy striving is self-focused: How can I improve? Perfectionism is other-focused: What will they think? Perfectionism is a hustle.

---

[*] For more, see *The Gifts of Imperfection: Let Go of Who You Think You're Supposed to Be and Embrace Who You Are.* Copyright © 2010 by Brené Brown. Center City, MN: Hazeldon.

- Perfectionism is not the key to success. In fact, research shows that perfectionism hampers achievement. Perfectionism is correlated with depression, anxiety, addiction, and life paralysis or missed opportunities. The fear of failing, making mistakes, not meeting people's expectations, and being criticized keeps us outside of the arena where healthy competition and striving unfolds.

- Last, perfectionism is not a way to avoid shame. Perfectionism is a form of shame. Where we struggle with perfectionism, we struggle with shame.

From her research, Dr. Brown developed the following definition of *perfectionism:*

- Perfectionism is a self-destructive and addictive belief system that fuels this primary thought: *If I look perfect and do everything perfectly, I can avoid or minimize the painful feelings of shame, judgment, and blame.*

- Perfectionism is self-destructive simply because perfection doesn't exist. It's an unattainable goal. Perfectionism is more about perception than internal motivation, and there is no way to control perception, no matter how much time and energy we spend trying.

- Perfectionism is addictive, because when we invariably do experience shame, judgment, and blame, we often believe it's because we weren't perfect enough. Rather than questioning the faulty logic of perfectionism we become even more entrenched in our quest to look and do everything just right.

- Perfectionism actually sets us up to feel shame, judgment, and blame, which then leads to even more shame and self-blame: "It's my fault. I'm feeling this way because I'm not good enough."[*]

Perfectionists tend to be very critical and judgmental, especially regarding themselves. They often engage in irrational thinking, applying rigid and unrealistic expectations to everything they do. All-or-nothing thinking is common.

---

[*] From *Daring Greatly: How the Courage to Be Vulnerable Transforms the Way We Live, Love, Parents, and Lead* by Brené Brown. Copyright © 2012 by Brené Brown. Used by permission of Gotham Books, an imprint of Penguin Group (USA) LLC.

For example, "If I'm not perfect, I must be terrible," "If I mess up, I must be incompetent," or "If I'm always perfect, people will like and respect me." Minimization and magnification are also used to discredit accomplishments and instead focus on shortcomings. For example, "I finished the race but I didn't win" or "Nobody will like me because I'm not the best." Perfectionists sometimes extend their rigid standards to seemingly simple tasks. For example, it's not enough just to shovel a clear path in the driveway; all of the snow must be perfectly removed. Laundry must be folded into perfectly neat piles. Doing a half-assed job is never acceptable under any circumstances. Anything less than perfect results in feelings of unworthiness and failure.

Perfectionists often fail to meet personal expectations because the criteria they set are so inflexible. They then focus on what was *not* accomplished rather than what was. Perfectionists tend to be self-depreciating and self-punishing. They derive self-worth from being perfect; but, because perfection is impossible, the perfectionist will often be left with feelings of unworthiness and damaged self-esteem. Low self-esteem creates an even stronger urge to obtain perfection in order to boost feelings of self-worth. Thus, perfectionism and low-self esteem become a vicious cycle.

Perfectionists may also struggle with procrastination and decision-making. Because they are afraid of making choices that are anything less than perfect, perfectionists often delay or avoid making decisions altogether. They often rely on others to make decisions, even including choices that seem fairly simple, such as which restaurant to go to for lunch. This inability to choose or voice an opinion can create a weakened personal identity and a diminished sense of self-worth.

Characteristics of Perfectionists

In *On the Wings of Self-Esteem,* Dr. Louise Hart lists the following characteristics exhibited by perfectionists:[*]

- Their impossible expectations constrict and inhibit their expression, stifle their creativity, and set them up for failure. They are frequently frustrated, disappointed, and angry.

- No matter how successful they are, they are seldom satisfied, they rarely appreciate their achievements or give themselves a pat on the back.

- They don't feel "good enough."

- They are rigid and controlling of themselves—and others.

---

[*] Copyright © 1994 by Dr. Louise Hart, from *On the Wings of Self-Esteem.* Oakland, CA: Uplift Press. Reprinted by permission of Uplift Press.

- They don't try, don't start, procrastinate, or don't finish projects.

- Mistakes, to perfectionists, are proof of total failure; they can devastate self-esteem.

- They are judgmental and critical of themselves and of everyone else.

- They always focus on what is wrong—the shortcomings, flaws, and imperfections—and miss all the things that are "right."

- They have difficulty with decisions because they're trying to make a "perfect" decision.

- Entangled in trivia, they can't see the big picture. They usually end up doing all the work themselves because no one else can do it "just right."

- Either-or thinking is common; as one woman learned from her mother, "You are perfect or you are nothing." Perfectionists don't know how much room there really is between "perfect" and "total failure."

- Focusing on appearances, they miss the rich, internal dimensions of life. Instead of just allowing her feelings when her husband died, one woman ran out and bought several etiquette books on the subject so she could grieve "perfectly."

Other Consequences of Perfectionism

In addition to affecting the individual's self-esteem and creating feelings of frustration and disappointment, perfectionism can also have a negative impact on relationships. Perfectionists often seek to obtain intimacy and approval through appearing perfect at all times. A perfectionist doesn't believe that others will accept her flaws and imperfections; thus, she puts on a façade, hiding her true self from others. This tendency to maintain a front limits closeness in relationships. In reality, people actually tend to feel uncomfortable around those who appear too perfect because they often seem unapproachable, closed-off, or fake.

Perfectionists may be viewed as controlling, inflexible, or mean-spirited due to their rigid standards. This can create tension and conflict in all types of relationships, including those with family, friends, and co-workers, and even with various strangers you encounter throughout the day, such as customer service representatives, store clerks, and restaurant servers.

The roots of perfectionism tend to develop over time and can often be traced to the messages in our culture that we began witnessing in childhood and incorporated into our thinking as we were growing up. Our society is filled with media and advertising that portray unrealistic standards of existence. For example, airbrushed and photoshopped models in the majority of commercials and magazines, or the indication that we are supposed to be multitasking superheroes, easily juggling all of our personal, family, and career responsibilities. We need to recognize these standards as unrealistic and begin to let go of the perfectionist desire to measure up.

In your childhood, you may have received messages that created a foundation of perfectionism. Instead of receiving recognition for your inherent worth as a person and appropriate guidance from caretakers as you were growing up, you may have encountered too much criticism, creating a constant quest for approval. Your caretakers may have held expectations or set goals that were poorly defined or too accelerated, or you may have received praise only for major accomplishments, while values such as effort and perseverance were overlooked.

In *Self-Compassion: Stop Beating Yourself Up and Leave Insecurity Behind,* Kristin Neff says, "People with critical parents learn the message early on that they are so bad and flawed that they have no right to be accepted for who they are." Many perfectionists can recall hearing messages such as, "Good report card, but why did you get a B instead of an A in math?" Or "Great game, but why did you miss that shot in the second half?" These types of backhanded compliments foster shame and create the foundation for perfectionism and low self-esteem.

Regardless of the roots of your perfectionist tendencies, learning to let go of the need to be perfect will help you to feel more happy and fulfilled in the long run. It's okay to have goals and to strive to do your best, but the motivation for doing so should not be tied to your feelings of self-worth. It is important to accept imperfection and recognize that mistakes are how we learn and grow.

The long-term consequence of perfectionism is burnout. Eventually, perfectionists deplete themselves to the point that their physical and mental resources become exhausted. You can begin to let go of your perfectionist tendencies by first identifying what they are and why they persist. It involves picking apart the faulty messaging behind the *need* to be perfect and choosing to let go of irrational, distorted beliefs as you instead begin to incorporate more rational and realistic messages about yourself and the world into your daily thinking.

Identifying Perfectionist Thoughts

Perfectionism is caused by distorted thinking that often involves an underlying sense of fear. Common fears include fear of failure, fear of not being accepted or liked, or fear of being viewed as inadequate. To begin exploring the origin of your perfectionist tendencies, complete the following sentence:

If I'm not perfect, _____

_____

_____

_____

_____

Are you able to identify any faulty thinking or unrealistic standards in your answer? How can you change your answer to something more rational?

In *Overcoming Perfectionism: Finding the Key to Balance & Self-Acceptance*, Ann W. Smith distinguishes between overt and covert perfectionists and provides the following lists to help test the degree of perfectionism in an individual. Most people have a few positive responses, but if you check three or more items on two out of three tests, this may be an indication that you will want to work on perfectionism.

Self-Tests[*]

Test 1: General Perfectionism
- I place excessive demands on myself.
- I often obsess about the details of a task, even though they may not be important.
- I have trouble letting go of something once I have finished it (e.g., a project, a writing assignment, a paint job, a letter, taxes, or a cleanup job).
- I get very upset with myself when I make a mistake.
- I get more upset when I make a mistake and someone sees it.

- I often have a mental list of things I "should" be doing.
- I never seem to be doing enough.
- I tend to notice any error in myself or others before I notice the positive.
- I am very upset by criticism.
- I get defensive when I am corrected or criticized.
- I have difficulty making decisions.
- I get upset if I have to learn something new and I don't catch on quickly.

Test 2: Overt Perfectionists
- I rarely make mistakes.
- I tend to criticize or complain about the way other people do things.
- People say I am too "together" (e.g., uptight, or neat).
- I am annoyed when others don't act or behave as well as I think they should (e.g., in being on time or keeping order).
- Others would describe me as a perfectionist.
- My surroundings are generally in good order.
- I feel frustrated when my home is cluttered.
- I prefer routine and structure.
- I am very organized in one or more areas of my life.
- I sometimes wish I could just let go and relax.
- I have an all-or-nothing philosophy: If I can't do it all, or do it well, why bother?
- I am sometimes hard on the people around me.

Test 3: Covert Perfectionists
- I procrastinate on tasks that require a lot of effort.
- I am very hard on myself when I make mistakes.
- I feel terrible when anyone sees me make a mistake.
- I consider myself to be laid-back.
- I am critical of myself in my head.
- I think a lot about what I should be doing.
- I don't usually measure up to what I think I should be.
- I am not interested in being the best at most things.
- When I am good at something, I try harder.
- I tend to avoid things that I may not be good at.
- I often believe that people don't think highly of me.
- Others say that I am better than I think of myself.
- I underestimate my abilities at many things.

If many of the above statements are true for you, recognize that you have perfectionist tendencies; however, don't beat yourself up for this. Watch out for negative self-talk around belittling yourself for perfectionist ways and instead recognize that perfectionism is common and is something you can work to overcome. If you blame yourself for having perfectionist tendencies, you will only reinforce low self-esteem. Your perfectionism may even worsen as your bad feelings about yourself increase and you feel an even greater need to be perfect to compensate. Instead of blaming yourself, recognize and accept that you have perfectionist tendencies and commit to working to overcome them.

Start by making peace with your imperfections and weaknesses. Accept yourself as you are and let go of any self-destructive patterns and unrealistic expectations you hold yourself to. It is okay to have goals and standards for yourself, but it is unrealistic and unproductive to expect perfection.

Begin incorporating into your thinking messages that counter perfectionism; for example, sentences like, "I do not have to be perfect" and "I do the best I can." Say these sentences over and over anytime you feel pulled toward perfection or find yourself fixating on shortcomings.

Guidelines for Overcoming Perfectionism

In *The Anxiety & Phobia Workbook* (4th edition), Dr. Edmund J. Bourne suggests the following guidelines to help with overcoming perfectionism:

- Let Go of the Idea That Your Worth Is Determined by Your Achievements and Accomplishments…
- Recognize and Overcome Perfectionist Thinking Styles…
- Stop Magnifying the Importance of Small Errors…
- Focus on Positives…
- Work on Goals That Are Realistic…
- Cultivate More Pleasure and Recreation in Your Life…
- Develop a Process Orientation.[*]

As you develop an understanding of inherent self-worth, begin reinforcing the idea that you have worth simply because you are a human being. Work to recognize that worth is not determined by your achievements or accomplishments. Rely on yourself, rather than on society and others' messages, to determine your self-worth.

Become aware of your self-talk and pay attention to your distorted thinking and mistaken beliefs, especially as they relate to perfectionist thinking styles. Look out for should statements, all-or-nothing thinking, overgeneralization, and minimization/magnification. Create counterstatements and affirmations that refute perfectionist messages. Recognize that mistakes are how we learn. Work on

---

[*] Copyright © 2005 *The Anxiety & Phobia Workbook* (4th ed.) by Bourne, Edmund J. Reproduced with permission of New Harbinger Publications in the format Republish in a book via Copyright Clearance Center.

forgiving yourself and accept that having some shortcomings is natural. Beware of the tendency to magnify flaws and errors.

Focus on positives, including baby steps and little victories. Take an inventory of the "good" things you have accomplished each day. Watch out for the tendency to disqualify something positive with a "but." For example, "I got my chores done *but* I didn't have time to make dinner." Also recognize positives that may seem minor. Sometimes it's enough to just say, "I made it through a tough day."

Pay attention to whether your goals and expectations are realistic and obtainable. Again, watch out for should statements and for words like *always* and *never*. It is often helpful to set goals that are fairly easy and gradually raise the bar over time. This helps to keep you motivated rather than set you up for failure and discouragement. For example, if you set a goal to exercise seven days a week, your perfectionism will lead to disappointment and beating yourself up if you only exercise six days one week. Instead, set a goal to exercise two or three days a week. This goal is much more obtainable and allows some flexibility for days when you do not find the time or energy to workout. When you accomplish your goal, you will feel good about yourself and motivated to continue, thus able to raise the bar rather than quit.

Perfectionism creates the tendency to be rigid and self-denying. Becoming so wrapped up in striving for perfection and in focusing on failures causes the positive aspects of life to be overlooked, taken for granted, or forsaken. Try to relax your standards and make an attempt to add recreation, pleasure, and fun back into your life.

Developing a process orientation means beginning to consider that the *effort* you put into things is just as important as the outcome. Recognize that things like motivation, hard work, practice, and perseverance are significant and admirable, even when the end result is less than perfect.

Recommended Journaling

Perfectionism

Consider whether you have any perfectionist tendencies. Do you set too high of standards for yourself in any areas? Are you able to accept your shortcomings, weaknesses, and mistakes?

If you can identify any perfectionist tendencies in yourself, consider how they have affected you and your life. How have they affected other people in your life? How much time has trying to be perfect taken up? How has it affected the way you feel about yourself?

What would happen if you lowered your standards by some percentage? When developing an answer, rely on rational thinking and be aware of any mistaken, irrational, or distorted beliefs that creep into your thinking.

5

Thought-Stopping & Replacing Negative Self-Talk

Questions to Consider

- Have you ever tried to block out negative thoughts you have had about yourself?

- If so, did you find it difficult to do?

- What gets in the way of stopping or shutting out the negative voice inside your head?

- Have you ever considered that talking more kindly to yourself could have a dramatic impact on how you feel? Have you tried it? If so, what happened?

Thought-Stopping & Replacing Negative Self-Talk

Now that we've defined negative self-talk and identified the various ways it can show up, let's talk about how we can begin to break the habit of engaging in these destructive ways of thinking. The first step in changing unhealthy thinking involves developing awareness. You've gained a better understanding of the different types of negative thinking and already have a greater awareness of how harmful these messages can be. When you gain an understanding of how negative self-talk messages can show up and affect you through your everyday thought processes, you naturally become more aware of what's going on inside your head. This awareness alone lays the foundation for change. Moving forward, you will likely be more cognizant of times you are engaging in negative self-talk. It will also be important to actively start monitoring your daily thinking and to begin using a tool called *Thought-Stopping.*

Thought-stopping is a technique used to help catch the negative messages and distorted thoughts going through our minds. As you begin to catch these negative messages, you can work to change them into more positive, self-nurturing messages. Changing the way you think can ultimately change the way you feel and can improve your self-esteem.

Thought-Stopping Step One: Identifying the Thought

The first step in changing the way you think is to monitor your current thoughts and identify any negative messages. Throughout your day, become really aware of what you are thinking at any given moment. When something happens, pay attention to the messages or thoughts that go through your head. This can be challenging at first, because we are so used to going about our day without really stopping to consider what thoughts are racing through our minds. Make an effort to really notice what you are thinking.

Often, it is helpful to start with a feeling. For example, if you notice you are feeling upset, then stop and consider what you are thinking. There is always a thought behind a feeling. If you notice you are angry, stop and really think about the thought behind the anger. For some people, the first sign may be a physical sensation, such as an upset stomach or tension in certain muscles. As you learn to identify thoughts as they relate to feelings or physical sensations, you will likely notice a pattern. Over time, it will become easier to catch this negative thinking as soon as it occurs.

When you do recognize that you are engaging in negative self-talk, try to formulate the thought into a sentence. At first, it may be helpful to write down some of the statements or sentences that form the underlying thoughts. Doing so will help you to see the actual thought more clearly and will make it easier to identify any self-defeating or irrational thoughts that creep into your self-talk.

As you start to identify your thoughts and pick apart your thinking, you will likely realize that many of the thoughts include negative self-talk, distorted thinking, and self-defeating beliefs. It is important to stop these thoughts right in their tracks. A participant in one of my workshops offered a great visual aid to conceptualize this: She referred to catching negative thoughts as "pulling mind-weeds." If you are a visual person, it may help to imagine yourself plucking the negative messages from your mind one by one. Other visuals that can be helpful include imagining a big red stop sign, a giant X, or a slamming door.

Some people find it helpful to also use something tangible to help emphasize times when they discover they are thinking negatively. For example, many people advocate wearing a rubber band around your wrist and snapping it each time you catch yourself engaging in negative self-talk. Others find it helpful (and less painful!) to say "STOP" out loud or to clap in front of their face when they notice they are using negative self-talk.

As you begin to practice identifying negative self-talk, try various tools to help you fine-tune the process and determine what is most helpful for you. Expect it to be challenging at first and be patient with yourself. The more you practice thought-stopping, the easier it will become.

Thought-Stopping Step Two: Replace the Thought

Once you've become able to identify dysfunctional thoughts, the next step is to begin replacing them with sentences that are less harsh and more positive and realistic. For example, if you catch yourself thinking, "I'm a loser," recognize that you are labeling yourself and then change the thought to something less severe; for example, "I made a mistake, but that doesn't mean I'm a bad person." If you catch yourself thinking, "Everybody at work thinks I'm stupid and worthless," change this to something more rational, such as, "Everybody at work doesn't have to like me. I know that I am competent at my job." The goal is to lessen self-disparaging thoughts by replacing them with sentences that are kinder, more accepting, and more in line with healthy self-talk.

Healthy / Positive / Rational Self-Talk

Healthy self-talk includes messages that are positive (or at least neutral), rational, realistic, and supportive, rather than self-depreciating. Sentences used to counter negative self-talk do not need to be over the top or the complete opposite of the negative thought. They don't need to be glowing, exaggerated, or overly positive. They just need to be rational and not rejecting. For example, if the negative thought is, "I'm stupid," the rational thought does not need to be "I'm the smartest person ever," or even "I am smart." It can be something neutral like, "I'm not great at math, but there are a lot of other things I'm good at," "Everyone makes mistakes," or simply, "I am okay."

Stopping the negative voice and instead inserting a positive, neutral, or rational statement helps prevent you from slipping into a downward spiral that includes self-bashing, damaged self-esteem, and feelings of depression and anxiety. At first, working to change self-talk from unhealthy to healthy may be difficult but, with practice, it will become easier. Since thinking of rational counterstatements may be difficult on the spot or while being flooded with negative emotions, it may be helpful to have a few key phrases memorized that you can recite when necessary. My favorite is simply "I'm okay," since it is useful in most any situation.

In *Therapist's Guide to Clinical Intervention: The 1-2-3's of Treatment Planning* (2nd edition), Sharon Johnson provides the following examples of rational/positive self-talk messages that may be useful in countering negative thinking:

Realistic Self-Talk[*]

- This too shall pass and my life will be better.
- I am a worthy and good person.
- I am doing the best I can, given my history and level of current awareness.
- Like everyone else, I am a fallible person and at times will make mistakes and learn from them.
- What is, is.
- Look at how much I have accomplished, and I am still progressing.
- There are no failures, only different degrees of success.
- Be honest and true to myself.
- It is okay to let myself be distressed for a while.
- I am not helpless. I can and will take the steps needed to get through this crisis.
- I will remain engaged and involved instead of isolating and withdrawing during this situation.
- This is an opportunity, instead of a threat. I will use this experience to learn something new, to change my direction, or to try a new approach.
- One step at a time.
- I can stay calm when talking to difficult people.
- I know I will be okay no matter what happens.

- He/She is responsible for their reaction to me.
- This difficult/painful situation will soon be over.
- I can stand anything for a while.
- In the long run, who will remember, or care?
- Is this really important enough to become upset about?
- I don't really need to prove myself in this situation.
- Other people's opinions are just their opinions.
- Others are not perfect, and I won't put pressure on myself by expecting them to be.
- I cannot control the behaviors of others, I can only control my own behaviors.
- I am not responsible to make other people okay.
- I will respond appropriately, and not be reactive.
- I feel better when I don't make assumptions about the thought or behaviors of others.
- I will enjoy myself, even when life is hard.
- I will enjoy myself while catching up on all I want to accomplish.
- Don't sweat the small stuff—it's all small stuff.
- My past does not control my future.
- I choose to be a happy person.
- I am respectful to others and deserve to be respected in return.
- There is less stress in being optimistic and choosing to be in control.
- I am willing to do whatever is necessary to make tomorrow better.

Using healthy self-talk is really about nurturing yourself. Think about the way you would treat a young child or a close friend, then make an effort to treat yourself the same way. Think about it—most of us would never talk to a child or a friend the way we talk to ourselves. So why don't we treat ourselves with the same respect we give to others? The one person you spend 100 percent of your time with is you, so make an effort to start treating yourself in a kinder manner. Stop when you catch yourself engaging in negative or distorted self-talk. Instead, give yourself positive, loving, and encouraging messages. Doing so is like holding up a shield or creating a protective wall against negative self-talk.

If you find talking to yourself in a loving way to be difficult, it may be useful to think about what you would say to a close friend if you heard him/her engaging in negative self-talk. Or it may be helpful to imagine that the person delivering the positive message is someone outside of yourself—a friend, mentor, or a loved one. Sometimes paying attention to self-talk and countering negative messages feels like the old cartoons that depict the devil on one shoulder and the angel on the other. It may feel a little ridiculous to talk to yourself from two different perspectives, but eventually, with practice, the good voice will overpower the negative one and will form your new norm of thinking.

A visual image that helps me conceptualize the ideas of self-esteem, self-talk, and damaging versus healthy messages, also borrowed from Ed Jacobs's *Creative Counseling Techniques*, is this: Imagine that a Styrofoam cup is your "Self-Esteem Cup." Each time you think a negative or distorted thought, it's like poking a hole in the cup. Your self-esteem begins to leak out. The more negative messages, the more holes, and the lower your self-esteem becomes. Positive self-talk statements serve to plug up and repair the holes, allowing you to hold on to and maintain your self-esteem. At first it will take a lot of positive messages to repair the damage and refill the holes that have been created from years of self-bashing. But remember that repetition rewires the brain and creates new habits. With time and practice, positive self-talk will become easier and will be more the norm, thus you won't have to work so hard to fix the damage created by negative self-talk messages. Thinking rationally will become more natural and will allow you to preserve your self-esteem.

Thought-Stopping Step Three: Praise Yourself!

The third step in thought-stopping involves praising yourself! Changing the pattern of negative thinking is difficult and it takes a lot of practice. Each time you are able to recognize negative self-talk and then change it to something more positive, you are taking a step toward changing your overall pattern of thinking. You are ultimately working to improve the way you feel and to increase your self-esteem. Praise yourself when you are able to recognize and stop a negative thought, and praise yourself again when you are able to change this thought into something more positive and rational. By giving yourself praise, you are beginning to create a healthy habit of positive and encouraging self-talk.

Thought-Changing Log

When you are first starting to practice thought-stopping and thought-changing, it may be useful to write the thoughts down. Putting thoughts down on paper helps you to hone in on the specific sentences that form negative thoughts and allows you to identify patterns in negative thinking. Writing down the rational response can help to give the new thought more power, especially if you read this new sentence on a regular basis.

Utilizing a chart, such as the one on the next page, can help you to track your negative thoughts, create rational responses, and pinpoint the outcomes as you begin monitoring your self-talk. Remember, it's often easier to catch negative thinking when you first start by identifying a negative emotion, such as anger, fear, or embarrassment.

Thought-Changing Log

Emotion(s)	Thought(s)	Rational Response	Outcome
Embarrassed	I am so stupid. I made a fool out of myself.	Everyone makes mistakes. The discomfort will pass.	I feel a little better. I protected my self-esteem.

Recommended Journaling

Thought-Stopping & Replacing Negative Self-Talk

As you become more skilled at catching negative self-talk, take things a step further by utilizing the "Thought-Changing Log" to track and reframe your unhealthy thoughts into something more neutral. Throughout the course of the next week, pay attention to times when you experience a negative emotion. Stop and identify your specific thoughts. Formulate them into sentences and notice what type of dysfunctional or unhealthy thinking is occurring. Write the thoughts down, consider where they come from, then work to dispute them with responses that are rational and nonjudgmental.

In your journal, write about how the thought-changing log works for you. Is it helpful? What did you find challenging? What successes are you experiencing with thought-stopping and thought-changing? Do you see any patterns or specific categories of distorted thinking occurring? Were you able to change any irrational beliefs or unhealthy statements into more positive ones? If so, what was the result? If not, what do you think stands in your way? Are there certain thoughts that are harder to dispute than others? Do you get caught up in berating yourself through "yeah but" responses during your attempts to think rationally? If so, make an attempt to cut yourself more slack. Overall, do you notice a greater awareness in terms of monitoring self-talk? If so, give yourself credit for taking the first step toward changing an old, destructive habit.

6

Affirmations

Questions to Consider

- Are you familiar with the term "affirmations" and have you ever heard of the "Law of Attraction"? If so, what is your understanding of these concepts?

- How often do you give yourself compliments, praise, pep talks, or encouragement? What types of things do you tend to say?

- Have you ever observed how you feel after receiving words of encouragement from yourself or others?

- Have you ever noticed that people who seem very happy, upbeat, and confident generally always have nice and positive things to say?

Affirmations

In addition to using positive messages to counter negative self-talk, it is also important to begin forming an underlying pattern of healthy self-talk by adding in positive, encouraging, and optimistic statements to your daily thinking. As you are breaking the bad habit of negative self-talk through thought-stopping and thought-replacing, you can also be forming the foundation for positive self-talk by ensuring you are thinking and talking to yourself in a positive manner on a regular basis, not only when countering negative thoughts. When your self-esteem is low, it can take ten or more positive comments for each negative in order to balance things out and protect self-esteem from further destruction. Therefore, it is important to start feeding yourself positive messages as often as possible.

Positive self-talk messages are sometimes referred to as *affirmations* or *mantras*. Affirmations are constructive, encouraging statements that are used to foster positivity in one's life. They can help you to change or avoid self-defeating thinking or mistaken beliefs. They help you to feel better about yourself and about various situations in your life. In order to build self-esteem, it will be necessary to start saying affirmations to yourself on a regular basis. The idea is that you want to bombard yourself with positive self-talk messages in order to overpower the years of negative self-talk that you have endured. (For an interesting description on some differences between affirmations and mantras, see *The Practice: Simple Tools for Managing Stress, Finding Inner Peace, and Uncovering Happiness* by Barb Schmidt.)

By repeating affirmations over and over, you begin to change how you think. You may have heard of the Law of Attraction, which basically says that positive thoughts are magnets for positive experiences. While some people criticize teachings on the Law of Attraction for taking the concept to the extreme in terms of talking about thoughts leading to the manifestation of material things, the basic idea behind the law is often true. The energy in your thinking has a large impact on how you feel and how things in your life are going.

Affirmations are a major component in making the Law of Attraction work to your advantage. By stating positive self-talk affirmations, you essentially invite healthy self-esteem and positive feelings into your life. The positive messages in your affirmations ultimately become part of your core beliefs and begin to weaken irrational thinking. When you shift your core beliefs toward messages that are rational, positive, and self-loving, you ultimately shift your brain's core view of yourself and the world. Research shows that repetition can literally change and rewire the brain. By practicing affirmations on a regular basis, you can change your brain and your default way of thinking, ultimately improving your self-esteem and the overall way you feel.

At first, you may find it difficult to come up with and say affirmations to yourself. This is because you have been stuck in a pattern of negative self-talk and low self-esteem. Speaking positively can feel awkward, silly, or unnatural. It will take practice to begin incorporating affirmations into your life. Even if, initially, you do not 100 percent believe an affirmation, continue to repeat it over and over to yourself, and eventually it will become your reality.

Some people find it helpful to write their affirmations down on paper or to create a ritual of saying one or two affirmations every morning or at night before bed. It can be helpful to post your affirmations somewhere where you will see them often, such as on a Post-it note on your bathroom mirror, car dashboard, or refrigerator.

Affirmations should be written in the first person and in the present tense, even though they may not be happening yet. This gives them more power, hope, and validity, allowing them to more readily become your truth. Affirmations are most effective when they are personal and written in your own words; however, they can be difficult to formulate at first if your self-esteem is low. As you are working to form a habit of positive self-talk and affirmative thinking, it may be useful to check out various books and resources that give ideas on how to formulate positive messages.

Some examples of affirmations for self-esteem follow. There are also many useful resources out there that help foster positive, affirmative thinking, including inspirational books, daily affirmation email subscriptions, smartphone apps, decks of affirmation cards, calendars with daily positive messages, etc. Louise Hay is one of my favorite "affirmation gurus." You can access her daily affirmations at www.louisehay.com or www.healyourlife.com. You can also find links to some recommended resources here: www.meganmaccutcheon.com/selftalk

Examples of Affirmations

The following lists of affirmation examples are from Dr. Edmund J. Bourne's *The Anxiety & Phobia Workbook* (4th edition):

Affirmations for Self-Esteem[*]

What You Are

- I am lovable and capable.
- I fully accept and believe in myself just the way I am.
- I am a unique and special person. There is no one else quite like me in the entire world.
- I accept all the different parts of myself.
- I am already worthy as a person. I don't have to prove myself.
- My feelings and needs are important.
- It's okay to think about what I need.
- It's good for me to take time for myself.
- I have many good qualities.
- I believe in my capabilities and value the unique talents I can offer the world.
- I am a person of high integrity and sincere purpose.
- I trust in my ability to succeed at my goals.
- I am a valuable and important person, worthy of the respect of others.
- Others perceive me as a good and likable person.
- When other people really get to know me, they like me.
- Other people like to be around me. They like to hear what I have to say and know what I think.
- Others recognize that I have a lot to offer.
- I deserve to be supported by those people who care for me.
- I deserve the respect of others.
- I trust and respect myself and am worthy of the respect of others.
- I now receive assistance and cooperation from others.
- I'm optimistic about life. I look forward to and enjoy new challenges.
- I know what my values are and am confident in the decisions I make.
- I easily accept compliments and praise from others.
- I take pride in what I've accomplished and look forward to what I intend to achieve.
- I believe in my ability to succeed.
- I love myself just the way I am.

---

[*] Copyright © 2005. *The Anxiety & Phobia Workbook* (4th ed.) by Bourne, Edmund J. Reproduced with permission of New Harbinger Publications in the format Republish in a Book via Copyright Clearance Center.

- I don't have to be perfect to be loved.
- The more I love myself, the more I am able to love others.

If it feels too difficult or foreign to say sentences like this to yourself, start by including the phrase "I am learning to." For example:

What You Are Learning:

- I am learning to love myself more every day.
- I am learning to believe in my unique worth and capabilities.
- I am learning to trust myself (and others).
- I am learning to recognize and take care of my needs.
- I am learning that my feelings and needs are just as important as anyone else's.
- I am learning to ask others for what I need.
- I am learning that it's okay to say no to others when I need to.
- I am learning to take life one day at a time.
- I am learning to approach my goals one day at a time.
- I am learning to take better care of myself.
- I am learning how to take more time for myself each day.
- I am learning to let go of doubts and fear.
- I am learning to let go of worry.
- I am learning to let go of guilt (or shame).
- I am learning that others respect and like me.
  I am learning how to be more comfortable around others.
- I am learning to feel more confident in _____.
- I am learning that I have a right to _____.
- I am learning that it's okay to make mistakes.
- I am learning that I don't have to be perfect to be loved.
- I am learning to accept myself just the way I am.

Affirmations That Counter Common Mistaken Beliefs[*]

- I am responsible and in control of my life.
- Circumstances are what they are, but I can choose my attitude toward them.
- I am becoming prosperous. I am creating the financial resources I need.
- I am setting priorities and making time for what is important.

- Life has its challenges and its satisfactions—I enjoy the adventure of life. Every challenge that comes along is an opportunity to learn and grow.
- I accept the natural ups and downs of life.
- I love and accept myself the way I am.
- I deserve the good things in life as much as anyone else.
- I am open to discovering new meaning in my life.
- It's never too late to change. I am improving one step at a time.
- I am innately healthy, strong, and capable of fully recovering. I am getting better every day.
- I am committed to overcoming my condition. I am working on recovering from my condition.
- I can recover by taking small risks at my own pace.
- I am looking forward to the new freedom and opportunities I'll have when I'm fully recovered.
- I am learning to love myself.
- I am learning to be comfortable by myself.
- If someone doesn't return my love, I let it go and move on.
- I am learning to be at peace with myself when alone. I am learning how to enjoy myself when alone.
- I respect and believe in myself apart from others' opinions.
- I can accept and learn from constructive criticism.
- I'm learning to be myself around others. It's important to take care of my own needs.
- It's okay to be myself around others. I'm willing to be myself around others.
- I appreciate my achievements and am worth more than all of them put together.
- I am learning how to balance work and play in my life.
- I am learning there is more to life than success. The greatest success is living well.
- I am a unique and capable person just as I am. I am satisfied doing the best I can.
- It's okay to make mistakes. I'm willing to accept my mistakes and learn from them.
- I'm willing to allow others to help me. I acknowledge my need for other people.
- I am open to receiving support from others.
- I am willing to take the risk of getting close to someone.
- I am learning to relax and let go. I'm learning to accept those things I can't control.
- I am willing to let others assist me in solving my problems.
- When I love and care for myself, I am best able to be generous to others.
- I'm doing the best I can as a _____. (Optional: And I'm open to learning ways to improve.)
- It's okay to be upset when things go wrong.

- It's okay if I don't always have a quick answer to every problem.
- It's okay to make time to rest and relax.
- I do the best I can, and I'm satisfied with that.
- It's okay if I'm unable to always foresee everything.
- It's okay to be angry sometimes. I am learning to accept and express my angry feelings appropriately.
- I'm learning to be honest with others, even when I'm not feeling pleasant or nice.
- I believe that I am an attractive, intelligent, and valuable person.
- I am learning to let go of guilt.
- I believe that I can change. I am willing to change (or grow).
- The world outside is a place to grow and have fun.
- Worrying about a problem is the real problem. Doing something about it will make a difference for the better.
- I am learning (or willing) to trust other people.
- I am making a commitment to myself to do what I can to overcome my problem with _____.
- I am learning that it is okay to make mistakes.
- Nobody's perfect—and I'm learning (or willing) to go easier on myself.
- I'm willing to become (or learn to become) self-sufficient.
- I'm learning to let go of worrying. I can replace worrying with constructive action.
- I am learning, one step at a time, that I can deal with the outside world.
- I am inherently worthy as a person. I accept myself just the way I am.

The previous lists include several ideas for affirmations that will help with building self-esteem and creating a habit of thinking in more rational, positive, caring ways. People with difficulty accepting their own inherent worth or those with many irrational beliefs will benefit from reading over these lists on a regular basis. Use these examples as a basis for creating your own list of affirmations and work to write your own affirmations in your own words.

Recommended Journaling

Affirmations

In your journal, come up with a list of affirmations for yourself. It may be helpful to first create a list of accomplishments and things you are proud of. You can refer back to the pluses on your Self-Concept Inventory as a starting point. List any positive traits, accomplishments, or things you like about yourself, no matter how small they may seem. Turn this inventory into a list of positive, affirmative statements.

Add sentences to address any areas you are looking to improve in your life. Incorporate any statements you like from the lists of affirmation examples into your own list. Remember that affirmations don't necessarily have to be things you believe in the present moment. Rather, they can be things you hope will become true for you. Add as many affirmations as possible to your list, considering both things you feel good about now and things you hope will become true for you in the future.

Make a point to read your affirmation list out loud every day. Throughout your day, practice saying various affirmations to yourself—both randomly during times you feel fine and also at times when you need an extra boost because you are feeling sad, stressed, or bad about yourself. If you need extra help remembering affirmations, write them down in places where you will see them during your day; for example, in your planner or your wallet. If you find it very difficult to come up with and tell yourself affirmations, start simply with, "I am learning to give myself positive affirmations."

You may find it helpful to get in the habit of writing down or thinking each night about one positive thing you did that day. Praise yourself for one accomplishment, even if it is simply making it through a stressful or boring day. "I made it through the day" is a positive self-talk message and has a much better effect on self-esteem than do thoughts like, "I didn't do anything worthwhile today" or "I can't think of anything positive."

Continue to pay attention to any negative messages that come into your mind and counter them with positive self-talk messages or shut them out with neutral affirmations. For example, if you start to think of something you messed up during the day, tell yourself, "I made a mistake and I am learning to accept that it is okay to make mistakes," or simply say out loud, "I am an okay person."

Self-Concept Inventory Revisited:

Refer back to your Self-Concept Inventory. It can provide an overview of what you currently view as strengths and weaknesses and can be a useful starting point for building a list of affirmations and seeing areas where thought-stopping and thought-revising may be necessary.

Review the items that you marked as positives and actively acknowledge your strengths. You can use these items to begin building affirmations by writing the positive traits into complete sentences. For example, refer back to the example of Eleanor's Self-Concept Inventory. She could take positive items from the "How I Relate to Others" section and formulate the following affirmations: "I am a warm and open person" and "I am a good communicator and a good listener."

Next, review the list of negatives and see whether you can revise this list. In *Self-Esteem: A Proven Program of Cognitive Techniques for Assessing, Improving, & Maintaining Your Self-Esteem* (3rd edition), Matthew McKay and Patrick Fanning list the following rules for revising items on your weakness list:

1.) Use non-pejorative language…
2.) Use accurate language…
3.) Use language that is specific rather than general. Eliminate words like everything, always, never, completely, and so on…
4.) Find exceptions or corresponding strengths.[*]

For example, refer back to Eleanor's Self-Concept Inventory. When Eleanor revised the weaknesses on her list, she changed "Buckteeth" to "Prominent front teeth" and "Ugly nose" to "Proportionately too-large nose." She changed "Phony with friends" to "Reluctant to express anger with friends" and "Know nothing" to "Know little about current events or history; don't read the newspaper. Know a lot about psychology, pharmaceutical, children, modern dance, making a family work."

Weaknesses or items you view as flaws can also help to pinpoint things you hope to change or need to learn to accept. Affirmations can be created to help you to improve weak areas or assist you in making peace with your shortcomings. For example, from the statements "Can't set limits or say no" and "Can't ask for what I want," Eleanor could create the following affirmation: "I am learning to be more assertive." If Eleanor frequently focuses on the negative aspects of her physical appearance (fat belly, fat thighs, flat chested), it would be useful for her to create an affirmation to the effect of: "I accept and appreciate my body."

Although we will all have some weaknesses in various areas of ourselves, we can protect our self-esteem by eliminating critical language and negative labels, and by viewing these areas in a more realistic manner. If you find yourself constantly ruminating over weaknesses or having difficulty shutting out the negative self-talk, get into the habit of frequently repeating out loud a neutral affirmation, such as "I accept myself" or "I am learning to accept myself."

It will be easier to create affirmations for things you already see as positives than it will be for the areas you view as weaknesses; however, the negative areas will be the most important to concentrate on. Start with affirmations you are comfortable saying and gradually add in additional ones that address your areas of weakness. Remember you can use the words "I am learning to" in affirmations to help bridge the gap between a weakness and a positive statement you feel comfortable saying.

In *The Self-Esteem Companion: Simple Exercises to Help You Challenge Your Inner Critic and Celebrate Your Personal Strengths,* Matthew McKay, Patrick Fanning, Carole Honeychurch, and Catharine Sutker suggest using the affirmation, "Today I like myself more than yesterday. Tomorrow I will like myself more than today." This is a great affirmation for anyone working toward building self-esteem. The main goal in using affirmations to improve self-esteem is to inundate yourself with healthy, rational, loving messages as much as possible to counter the impact of negative self-talk.

7

Self-Esteem & Relationships

Questions to Consider

- How do friends, family, and others in your life affect your self-esteem?

- How much time do you spend with those who have a negative impact on your self-esteem?

- How much time do you spend with people who model healthy self-esteem?

- Which friends or family members help you to boost self-esteem and which tend to bring you down?

- Growing up, were you accepted by others? Noticed and valued by others?

- How did family members communicate their thoughts and feelings about you as a person? Did you tend to feel acknowledged and loved? Or ignored and unimportant?

- What messages do you remember receiving about yourself and your roles within your family or peer group?

Self-Esteem & Relationships

As a human, you are born with inherent self-worth. Your *perception* of personal worth is shaped by various experiences that occur within the context of relationships. At a very young age, you begin to internalize the messages you receive from the ways in which you are treated by caregivers and important figures in your life. Through the interactions and responses of others, you give meaning to and draw conclusions about your own identity and value.

Those with emotionally stable, healthy, nurturing caregivers tend to receive messages that they are important, loved, and valued, thus they have a better chance of developing and maintaining a foundation of healthy, positive self-esteem. On the other hand, individuals with less nurturing or dysfunctional caretakers, or caretakers who themselves have low self-esteem, tend to receive confusing messages regarding their identity and self-worth, and are more susceptible to forming unhealthy self-esteem that includes patterns of negative self-talk and distorted thinking.

Self-talk and self-esteem can also be shaped by the things we witness in others regarding how they treat themselves. As children, we are constantly observing others and are influenced by the actions and behaviors they model. For example, if we witness our parents putting themselves down, we will likely also develop the tendency to be critical of ourselves. That is why it can be really damaging for parents to say out loud in front of their kids things like, "Oh, I'm such a dummy" or ask questions such as, "Do I look fat in these jeans?" These types of messages teach children to be self-critical and to focus on the negatives, which encourages negative self-talk that prohibits healthy self-esteem or ultimately lowers it over time. Similarly, many families convey the message that it is not okay to show emotions or share feelings. Since experiencing a range of emotions at various times is inevitable, this type of messaging can also create identity confusion and feelings of being fundamentally wrong.

As you grow and encounter new situations, your self-esteem is continuously impacted by your experiences and relationships, including those with relatives, teachers, peers, and friends. Self-esteem can change in either direction (positive or negative) through various experiences and through your interpretations of the things others do and say to you throughout your life. Self-esteem can be built up through positive relationships with peers, mentors, and significant others who encourage self-confidence and model healthy self-talk, or it can be torn apart by humiliating experiences, abusive relationships, or traumatic incidents that lead us to doubt our worth.

In *Self-Compassion: Stop Beating Yourself Up and Leave Insecurity Behind,* Kristin Neff says, "While most research into the origins of self-criticism focuses on parents, the truth is that constant criticism by *any* significant figure in a child's life—a grandparent, a sibling, a teacher, a coach—can lead that child to experience inner demons later on in life." Being treated poorly, and things like shame, ridicule, and labels, can shape and establish feelings of unworthiness and negative self-esteem. On the other hand, being treated with kindness and respect positively influences your sense of self-worth and helps you to build self-esteem, whether it happens early on through encouraging relationships, or later through the implementation of your own positive self-talk.

While the foundation of self-esteem begins to develop early on, it is something that requires ongoing attention throughout your life. Actively practicing tools like positive self-talk to maintain healthy self-esteem is essential in order to protect against the adverse experiences and challenging relationships we are all bound to face at one time or another. Even somebody with the most devoted parents and the healthiest self-esteem is vulnerable to its loss without actively guarding against its destruction through the use of self-talk that is rational and constructive rather than negative and damaging. For example, somebody with initially positive self-esteem can experience its loss if she gets involved in an emotionally abusive relationship, whether romantically or in another type of setting, where the dysfunctional dynamics and subtle power struggles make her begin to doubt her own self-worth. The concepts of a "thick skin" or "strong backbone" are often referenced in regard to dealing with critical people or taxing situations. Healthy self-esteem fueled by positive self-talk is precisely the thing necessary to protect against potentially harmful people and toxic relationships.

While it is often difficult to pinpoint specifically when and where negative self-esteem or negative self-talk began, there is a good chance that feelings of inadequacy may be linked to adverse interactions or encounters with others. Individuals with a negative self-image tend to have very specific memories that involve being shamed, embarrassed, put down, or reprimanded by a parent, teacher, or other significant figure. We tend to remember and give much more weight to the negative experiences that happened in our past. These negative experiences have a great impact on how we perceive ourselves and come to form an understanding of our core worth. They ultimately shape the way we talk to ourselves internally and treat ourselves on the whole. Sometimes, internal self-talk and the voices we hear inside our heads are a direct reflection of the messages we heard growing up or within a specific relationship. As you begin to consider what experiences and relationships impacted your self-esteem throughout your life, it is useful to think about what messages you received about yourself in your past.

Messages from the Past

Because our internal self-talk is often shaped by the things we witnessed or heard growing up, it is useful to think about what messages you received during your childhood and adolescence. These messages are sometimes loud and clear; for example, when a parent verbally tells you something positive, such as, "I love you," or something negative, like, "You will never amount to anything." Messages can also be more subtle and received through actions rather than words; for example, some parents send the message that they support and love their child by always showing up to important events, while other parents may send the message that their child is insignificant or not a priority if they consistently seem too busy to pay attention. During grade school, you may have received messages from teachers, coaches, or role models that your efforts and attempts were worthwhile. Conversely, you may have understood their negative interactions to mean your opinions and endeavors did not matter.

As you work to evaluate your own level of self-esteem, it can be useful to consider what messages you heard as a child about yourself and about the way your family, peers, teachers, and role models perceived you. By considering how their comments, compliments, criticisms, actions, and inactions may have affected you, you gain a better sense of how various experiences contributed to your current level of self-esteem. Think about what role various people played in terms of the development of your identity.

Examples of Messages from Childhood

Read through the list of messages below and check the ones that you recall frequently hearing (or feeling) growing up. Consider how these messages affect you and your opinions of yourself today.

- ☐ I like you.
- ☐ I love you.
- ☐ You are unconditionally lovable.
- ☐ I appreciate you.
- ☐ I trust you.
- ☐ You matter.
- ☐ I value you.
- ☐ I'm lucky to have you.
- ☐ I cherish my time with you.
- ☐ I want to take care of you.
- ☐ I want to help you.
- ☐ I will protect you.
- ☐ I am proud of you.
- ☐ I am thankful for you.
- ☐ You are wanted.
- ☐ You are smart.

- ☐ You are a priority.
- ☐ You are allowed to make mistakes.
- ☐ You are attractive.
- ☐ I'm here for you.
- ☐ I miss you when we are apart.
- ☐ You make me happy.
- ☐ You are fun to be around.
- ☐ You are huggable.
- ☐ You are nice.
- ☐ You are good.
- ☐ You are successful.
- ☐ You are important.
- ☐ You are not important.
- ☐ You don't matter.
- ☐ I wish you were never born.
- ☐ You are a disappointment.
- ☐ Go away.
- ☐ I'm too busy for you.
- ☐ Your needs are not important.
- ☐ You can't do anything right.
- ☐ You are unwanted.
- ☐ You are a burden.
- ☐ You are careless.
- ☐ You are not smart enough.
- ☐ You are not good enough.
- ☐ You are an embarrassment.
- ☐ I disapprove of your appearance.
- ☐ You are incompetent.
- ☐ You'll never amount to anything.
- ☐ You are at fault.
- ☐ You wear on my nerves.
- ☐ My love for you can end at any moment.
- ☐ You're a troublemaker.
- ☐ You're wrong.
- ☐ You're bad.
- ☐ You are not trusted.

☐ I don't like to be near you.

☐ Don't show your feelings.

☐ Negative emotions are not okay.

☐ You're a nuisance.

☐ You're selfish.

☐ It's your job to make me happy.

☐ I own you. I can do whatever I want with you.

While reading over the list, you may have related to several of the messages and this may have stirred up some feelings in you. You might identify with some of the positive as well as some of the negative statements. Often, we receive mixed messages from key people in our lives, or we receive different types of messages from different people. This can create identity confusion that prohibits the development of healthy self-esteem. In general, we tend to hold on to, remember, and be most affected by the negative or confusing experiences, comments, and memories from our pasts. Part of building self-esteem often involves letting go of the wounds we have suffered and choosing to instead embrace the positive aspects of ourselves in order to find self-love.

Low Self-Esteem Negatively Impacts Relationships

One consequence of maintaining unhealthy self-esteem is that it can negatively impact all of your current relationships. This means not only romantic relationships, but also the relationships you have at work, with friends, with your extended family, with your children, and even with acquaintances. Low self-esteem fosters behaviors that can lead to dysfunction in or the deterioration of relationships, creating problems like power imbalances or isolation. These things only serve to reinforce negative feelings and low self-esteem, creating a vicious cycle or downward spiral. When you are not able to respect or see yourself favorably, you are not able to have healthy connections with others. The idea that you cannot truly love others until you love yourself rings true.

When you have unhealthy self-esteem, your negativity is often apparent to others. Healthy, functional people generally feel uncomfortable around those who demonstrate low levels of self-esteem and who constantly put themselves down, while emotionally unhealthy or unstable people are often drawn to people who appear emotionally weaker. When your self-esteem is low, you become vulnerable to being taken advantage of within relationships. People with low self-esteem sometimes end up in relationships with individuals who are narcissistic, controlling, or abusive. The consequences of these relationships can devastate self-esteem even further.

In *Loving Him Without Losing You: Seven Empowering Strategies for Better Relationships,* Beverly Engel talks about the concept of the "disappearing woman" and describes how women who lack self-esteem, independence, and assertiveness tend to easily lose themselves in relationships. For example, have you ever found yourself trying to change or claiming to enjoy something you did not in order to please or attract another person? This tendency only reinforces unhealthy self-esteem as you lose sight of who you really are. People with healthy self-esteem are able to express their own unique interests, wants, and needs without shame, embarrassment, or fear of driving others away.

When you work to improve self-esteem, you will likely find that it has a positive effect on healthy relationships and helps to highlight the problems and dysfunction in unhealthy ones. Healthy relationships between people with healthy self-esteem include characteristics like respect, consistency, equality, acknowledgment, appreciation, empathy, reality, honesty, and open communication.

Moving Forward with Healthy Self-Esteem and Healthy Relationships

As you begin to establish a sense of independence and let go of damaging experiences from the past, you come to realize that the most important relationship you have that impacts self-esteem is the one you have with yourself. Even if you had dysfunctional, neglectful, or disapproving parents, or negative and abusive relationships throughout your life, you can begin to change the impact these experiences have had on your self-esteem. By recognizing that your worth is not determined by the opinions or treatment of others, you can instead come to understand that the way you treat yourself is what really matters. The one person you are with 100 percent of the time is yourself, so your own internal messages will have the greatest impact. By learning to value yourself and making an effort to implement tools like thought-stopping and affirmations, you can build self-esteem and improve your quality of life.

As you work to build self-esteem and explore the roots of your negative self-talk, you may find yourself becoming angry about past experiences or feeling resentment toward various people who you now view as failing to foster healthy self-esteem in you. It is important to experience and acknowledge these feelings. Feelings are not a choice, but what you do with them is. Take care not to let negative feelings overwhelm you or create further tension in relationships. It is often helpful to realize that poor communication and dysfunction in relationships are patterns that are typically passed down from generation to generation. Your parents and caretakers were likely doing the best they could, given the experiences they faced in their own lives. Words or actions that caused you hurt or shame may not have been intentionally malicious.

I like to remember one of my favorite quotes by Maya Angelou, which reads, "Do the best you can until you know better. When you know better, do better." Although your caretakers may have been unable to model or instill in you healthy self-esteem, you can use the knowledge you are now learning to create and improve healthy self-esteem within yourself.

It may also be necessary to consider the role that religious or cultural beliefs play in the messages that you received and may continue to receive from various figures in your life. For example, American society values traits like independence, equality, and assertiveness, while other cultures may see these things as problematic. Your attempts to build self-esteem may be met with disapproval from others. This may be especially true for women whose cultural backgrounds include beliefs that women should not stand up for themselves, be independent, or make waves. It is useful to be aware of and acknowledge these obstacles and remember to respect the beliefs of others as you pursue the path that feels right for you.

If you find yourself struggling with negative feelings regarding your past or having difficulty integrating conflicting messages, it may be useful to seek individual therapy to help you explore and process how various experiences, relationships, interactions, beliefs, and values have impacted and shaped you. Some exercises for helping you to process these feelings will be presented in a later chapter.

Recommended Journaling

Self-Esteem & Relationships

In your journal, reflect upon how others affect your self-esteem. In what ways do various people in your life (at home, at work/school, friends, family members, etc.) affect your self-esteem, either negatively or positively? Who are the people who help you to feel good about yourself? Are there people who make you feel unworthy or inadequate?

How do you think your current level of self-esteem impacts others and your important relationships? What changes do you think you would see in your relationships if you were to develop a healthier level of self-esteem?

How do you think your family of origin impacted your self-esteem? Did they encourage the development of healthy, positive self-esteem or did their words or actions make it difficult to develop a positive self-identity? If your parents and caretakers were positive and nurturing influences, what got in the way of maintaining healthy self-esteem today? What other people or experiences in your life may have chipped away at your self-esteem throughout the years?

Create a list of the messages and labels you were given as a child. Make a conscious choice to hold on to the ones you like and those that build your self-esteem. Cross out the ones you wish to let go of and instead come up with a message that better fits how you see or would like to see yourself. Write down messages and labels you wish had been given to you in your childhood that would have helped you to feel good about yourself. Allow yourself to accept these ideas now. These positive messages can be turned into affirmations. Another affirmation you may wish to use is, "I am letting go of negative labels and hurtful messages from my past."

Boundaries

Questions to Consider

- Do you feel you have both a sense of independence as well as some interdependence with others?

- Do you frequently feel disrespected, put down, or taken advantage of?

- Do you find it difficult to set limits or enforce rules with others?

- Do you have a hard time saying no to others?

- Do you often look to other people to make choices and decisions for you?

Boundaries

As you are working to build self-esteem it will be important to pay close attention to your boundaries. The term "boundaries" refers to the rules and limits we set in our relationships with others. While a tangible boundary, such as a fence or wall, is fairly obvious and clear, personal boundaries are more abstract and not as easy to conceptualize. Yet, they are very important in terms of protecting yourself, both physically and emotionally.

You may have heard the concept "You teach others how to treat you." How others treat you is determined in part by your boundaries. If you have boundaries that are very healthy, well established, and clearly defined, others tend to treat you with respect because your boundaries demand it. Through healthy boundaries, you demonstrate a sense of self-respect and make it clear that you expect to be respected by others as well.

On the other hand, if your boundaries are weak, unclear, or nonexistent, you tend to be taken advantage of and treated poorly by others. Your weak boundaries send the message that you will tolerate being taken for granted or walked all over. Others do not give you the respect and consideration you inherently deserve.

Boundaries can be both verbal and nonverbal. Verbally, you can tell people what your expectations are, set limits, or give permission. Nonverbally, you can send messages via your body language, such as posture and facial expressions, or through your actions, such as engaging in or walking away from a situation or conversation. Physical boundaries establish who we choose to be near and who we allow to touch us. Emotional boundaries allow us to have our own feelings and to separate ourselves from people or situations that cause us discomfort. Mental or intellectual boundaries allow us to have our own thoughts, opinions, and ideas.

Boundaries tend to relate to how you feel about yourself. People with low self-esteem often have poor boundaries, whereas people with healthy self-esteem tend to have healthier boundaries. People with poor, unclearly defined boundaries often have their self-esteem chipped away at due to adverse encounters with others. It's kind of like the chicken and the egg: Which came first—poor boundaries or poor self-esteem? There is no clear answer, but the two go hand in hand and wind up reinforcing one another. When your boundaries are poor, you are vulnerable to being taken advantage of and disrespected. When you are repeatedly disrespected by others, you feel bad about yourself. Your negative self-talk may convince you that you do not deserve any better, thus, your self-esteem remains low and your boundaries remain poor, creating a vicious cycle.

Boundaries begin developing in early childhood as our caretakers send us messages (verbally, nonverbally, and through modeling) regarding how we should interact with and respond to others. These messages are incorporated with the messages we received about ourselves growing up and, together, they ultimately guide our boundaries. Those who grew up in families with dysfunctional dynamics, such as addiction, abandonment, abuse, or neglect, will likely have poorer boundaries and will have a more difficult time identifying and altering areas that need change; however, establishing appropriate boundaries is a necessary component to healthy self-esteem.

Sometimes boundaries can be very strict, rigid, or inflexible. People can become so set in their ways and adamant about certain things that they are unable to make adjustments to accommodate changes and differences. Boundaries that are too harsh or severe often lead to problems in interpersonal relationships. On the flip side, boundaries can also be too weak or very unclear. Poorly defined and unenforced boundaries can also lead to problems in relationships, as well as to difficulty protecting self-esteem. The healthiest boundaries are those that are somewhere in the middle: well-established and clear, yet flexible enough to adapt to various circumstances as necessary.

An example of unclear boundaries that is very common, especially in women, is the inability to ever say no. Somebody who has trouble saying no often fears hurting other people's feelings or making them angry. She may be worried about appearing selfish or uncaring, so she always says yes to things that are asked of her. This inability to say no can typically be traced to irrational thinking, such as, "If I voice my opinion, I will be seen as selfish and that will be terrible," or "If I say no I will appear coldhearted." Additionally, the inability to say no may relate to a failure to recognize and regard your own needs. Negative self-talk convinces you that your needs are unimportant or that expressing desires or requests will make you appear impolite or offensive, thus you are hesitant to communicate a boundary. When you are never able to say no, you run the risk of becoming overwhelmed and overworked, and of depleting your physical and emotional resources to the point of exhaustion and burnout. When your boundaries are weak, you do not take good care of yourself.

People with low self-esteem and a weak sense of self also tend to have a very difficult time making decisions. They habitually rely on others to take the lead or dictate choices. The problem stems from fear that a difference of opinion equals proof of wrongness or worthlessness. Even the simplest decisions, such as what type of food to eat or where to go for lunch, can seem overwhelming. The fear of speaking up and potentially having your ideas rejected can create intense feelings of anxiety. Your irrational thinking tells you that someone's rejection of your ideas or opinions must be proof that you are worthless. In the long run, the inability to make decisions and voice your own opinion conveys the message, to yourself and others, that your own wishes and needs are unimportant.

When you are unable to say no or voice your own opinions, you demonstrate weak boundaries. You tend to put everyone else first and you set the precedent that you will always be everything to everyone. You accommodate others, often at the expense and sacrifice of your own needs. Asking for help or speaking up to protect yourself may also be extremely difficult. Over time, the consequences of not expressing your own desires and needs include further diminished self-esteem and even weaker boundaries.

Another consequence of poor boundaries includes difficulties with interpersonal conflicts. People with unclear boundaries and low self-esteem are vulnerable to being taken advantage of. They may attract others who share a similar sense of poor boundaries but in the other extreme—those who have difficulty recognizing and respecting the wishes and boundaries of others. Aggressive people with poor boundaries have a hard time taking no for an answer and may end up being too pushy or forceful. Occasionally, those with poor boundaries demonstrate controlling and sometimes verbally or physically abusive behaviors. Developing a healthy sense of self-esteem with appropriate boundaries is vital to ensuring self-protection against these types of dysfunctional relationships.

Survey on Personal Boundaries

In *Boundaries and Relationships: Knowing, Protecting, and Enjoying the Self,* Charles L. Whitfield, M.D., offers the following questionnaire to help assess your own boundaries:

Survey on Personal Boundaries[*]

1.) I can't make up my mind.

    Never   Seldom   Occasionally   Often   Usually

2.) I have difficulty saying no to people.

    Never   Seldom   Occasionally   Often   Usually

3.) I feel as if my happiness depends on other people.

    Never   Seldom   Occasionally   Often   Usually

---

[*] Copyright © 1993 by Charles L. Whitfield, from *Boundaries and Relationships: Knowing, Protecting, and Enjoying the Self.* Deerfield Beach, FL: Health Communications, Inc. Reprinted by permission of Health Communications, Inc., www.hcibooks.com.

4.)   It's hard for me to look a person in the eyes.

       Never   Seldom   Occasionally   Often   Usually

5.)   I find myself getting involved with people who end up hurting me.

       Never   Seldom   Occasionally   Often   Usually

6.)   I trust others.

       Never   Seldom   Occasionally   Often   Usually

7.)   I would rather attend to others than attend to myself.

       Never   Seldom   Occasionally   Often   Usually

8.)   Others' opinions are more important than mine.

       Never   Seldom   Occasionally   Often   Usually

9.)   People take or use my things without asking me.

       Never   Seldom   Occasionally   Often   Usually

10.)   I have difficulty asking for what I want or what I need.

       Never   Seldom   Occasionally   Often   Usually

11.)   I lend people money and don't seem to get it back on time.

       Never   Seldom   Occasionally   Often   Usually

12.)   Some people I lend money to don't ever pay me back.

       Never   Seldom   Occasionally   Often   Usually

13.)   I feel ashamed.

       Never   Seldom   Occasionally   Often   Usually

14.) I would rather go along with another person or other people than express what I'd really like.

Never   Seldom   Occasionally   Often   Usually

15.) I feel bad for being so "different" from other people.

Never   Seldom   Occasionally   Often   Usually

16.) I feel anxious, scared, or afraid.

Never   Seldom   Occasionally   Often   Usually

17.) I spend my time and energy helping others so much that I neglect my own wants and needs.

Never   Seldom   Occasionally   Often   Usually

18.) It's hard for me to know what I believe and what I think.

Never   Seldom   Occasionally   Often   Usually

19.) I feel as if my happiness depends on circumstances outside of me.

Never   Seldom   Occasionally   Often   Usually

20.) I feel good.

Never   Seldom   Occasionally   Often   Usually

21.) I have a hard time knowing what I really feel.

Never   Seldom   Occasionally   Often   Usually

22.) I find myself getting involved with people who end up being bad for me.

Never   Seldom   Occasionally   Often   Usually

23.) It's hard for me to make decisions.

Never   Seldom   Occasionally   Often   Usually

24.) I get angry.

   Never   Seldom   Occasionally   Often   Usually

25.) I don't get to spend much time alone.

   Never   Seldom   Occasionally   Often   Usually

26.) I tend to take on the moods of people close to me.

   Never   Seldom   Occasionally   Often   Usually

27.) I have a hard time keeping a confidence or secret.

   Never   Seldom   Occasionally   Often   Usually

28.) I am overly sensitive to criticism.

   Never   Seldom   Occasionally   Often   Usually

29.) I feel hurt.

   Never   Seldom   Occasionally   Often   Usually

30.) I tend to stay in relationships that are hurting me.

   Never   Seldom   Occasionally   Often   Usually

31.) I feel an emptiness, as if something is missing in my life.

   Never   Seldom   Occasionally   Often   Usually

32.) I tend to get caught up "in the middle" of other people's problems.

   Never   Seldom   Occasionally   Often   Usually

33.) When someone I'm with acts up in public, I tend to feel embarrassed.

   Never   Seldom   Occasionally   Often   Usually

34.) I feel sad.

Never   Seldom   Occasionally   Often   Usually

35.) It's not easy for me to really know in my heart about my relationship with a Higher Power or God.

Never   Seldom   Occasionally   Often   Usually

36.) I prefer to rely on what others say about what I should believe and do about religious or spiritual matters.

Never   Seldom   Occasionally   Often   Usually

37.) I tend to take on or feel what others are feeling.

Never   Seldom   Occasionally   Often   Usually

38.) I put more into relationships that I get out of them.

Never   Seldom   Occasionally   Often   Usually

39.) I feel responsible for other people's feelings.

Never   Seldom   Occasionally   Often   Usually

40.) My friends or acquaintances have a hard time keeping secrets or confidences that I tell them.

Never   Seldom   Occasionally   Often   Usually

Boundaries Survey: Assessing and Scoring

In your answers to this survey, many responses of "Usually" and "Often" tend to indicate more boundary problems, distortions, or issues. These may also indicate some confusion over boundaries and limits, often called "blurred" or "fused" boundaries.

Persons who answered all or mostly "Never" may not be aware of their boundaries. A person who has healthy boundaries would tend to answer "Seldom" and sometimes "Occasionally." Rare items, like number 20, would be scored in the reverse.

Building Better Boundaries

As you work to build self-esteem, pay attention to the boundaries you convey to others and work to set limits that are well defined and protective of your well-being. The following guidelines are useful in establishing and maintaining healthy boundaries:

- Consider what your needs, wants, and desires are. Think about whether these things are currently being met in your life. If they are not, think about what stands in the way. Are there certain thoughts that convince you that your needs and wants are not important?

- Work on separating yourself from unhealthy situations and unhealthy relationships. You may need to distance yourself from toxic or abusive people. If you cannot distance yourself from certain people, utilize healthy, rational self-talk to remind yourself that you are not at fault and cannot control the behaviors of others. Using rational thinking and refraining from allowing the hurtful words and actions of others to negatively affect you helps to protect self-esteem.

- Ensure you have a healthy balance between independence and relying on others. Spend time with those who enrich your life, but also take time out to be alone.

- In relationships, be sure to maintain you own hobbies, friends, and interests. Do not lose sight of your own identity by being consumed with the relationship and constantly prioritizing the wishes and needs of others at the expense of your own. Be careful not to sacrifice your own desires and needs in favor of those of your friends/partner.

- Work on becoming aware of and accepting of your own thoughts, opinions, and emotions. Do not allow others to control your thinking or feelings. Don't give up your power by allowing others to make decisions for you.

- Make sure your actions and behaviors are in line with your own values and are not determined by the mandates or wishes of others.

- Work on setting limits with other people regarding what you are willing to accept and do.

- Create affirmations to help with establishing better boundaries; for example, "I protect and respect myself."

- Work on assertiveness (Chapter 10) to help enforce boundaries.

- Pay attention to times when you feel hurt or disrespected. Consider whether there are things you could have done to prevent or alter the situation if you had enforced better boundaries. Do not beat yourself up for poor boundaries but rather consider how you can improve or better enforce your boundaries in the future.

A Word of Caution About Boundaries

As you build self-esteem and begin to establish clearer, healthier boundaries, you will likely be met with initial resistance from those close to you. Although you are changing for the better, change is still very difficult for most people to accept. As you become healthier, the dynamics and the structure in your relationships will need to change to accommodate your new boundaries and improved self-esteem. This "rocking the boat" can pose a challenge to others, since they will need to make some changes as well. They may not like the fact that they have to modify the ways in which they interact with you. They may resent your improvements and the fact that you are no longer willing to be a doormat or a pushover. Be careful not to let this resistance discourage you from continuing your quest to build self-esteem. It can sometimes feel like two steps forward, one step back and harder before easier; however, if you stick with it, it will be worth it in the end.

When I think about boundaries and setting limits, I sometimes think of a scenario where a kid is screaming for candy in a candy store. If the parent says no but ultimately gives in and buys the child candy in order to end a tantrum, the parent's authority is undermined and it will be even harder to say no and be taken seriously in the future. If, however, the parents continues to firmly say no and refuse, despite the tantrum, the child will learn that no means no and future trips to the candy store will likely result in fewer power struggles and the parent's authority being respected more readily.

The ideal for setting boundaries is to be direct and firm the first time. If you give in, you set the precedent that you will cave under pressure. People will learn they can get away with ignoring what you say or pushing your boundaries, which makes it even harder to set limits and implement your authority. When you have a history of giving in or avoiding enforcing boundaries, it can be all the more difficult to create a new stance of good boundaries. Although the resistance or resentment of others will be a challenge in the beginning, the more you continue to enforce your new boundaries, the easier it will become for others to accept and ultimately respect them.

Recommended Journaling

Boundaries

How would you describe your boundaries with others? Do they tend to be too strict and rigid or too lax and unenforced? Are your boundaries different, or easier/harder to enforce with certain groups of people? Are there any current boundaries you are proud of or feel good about? Are there ones you wish existed or you wish you could better implement?

How do you make choices in your life? Do you rely on someone else to make or influence your decisions? Is it hard for you to voice your own opinions or ask for what you want? Do you find it hard to say no to others? Is there anyone in your life who you need to set stricter limits with?

How does your behavior toward others affect how they treat you? How do you think your boundaries with others may directly or indirectly affect your self-esteem? In your journal, create a list of affirmations that will help guide you in setting appropriate boundaries.

9

Criticisms & Compliments

Questions to Consider

- What is criticism? How does criticism affect your self-esteem? What are the differences between constructive criticism and destructive/shaming criticism?

- What are examples of compliments? How do they affect your self-esteem? Is it easy or difficult for you to accept compliments? Why?

- Did your family of origin and significant figures in your childhood tend to give you more compliments or more criticisms? Are there specific messages you remember today?

- Do you tend to hear more compliments or more criticisms from others in your life now?

Criticisms & Compliments

People with low self-esteem often have difficulty hearing, accepting, and responding well to both criticisms as well as compliments. Distorted thinking and negative self-talk allow critical comments to be taken personally, in a way that is destructive to self-esteem. People with low self-esteem and negative self-talk also tend to block compliments because the external validation conflicts with an internal sense of unworthiness.

In working to build self-esteem, it will be important to pay attention to how you handle critical or complimentary remarks from others. When you respond poorly to criticisms and compliments, the result is the reinforcement of low self-esteem. Working to respond more effectively to the evaluations of others can be another avenue to building and protecting self-esteem, while responding poorly can serve to further deplete it.

Criticisms

There are two different types of criticisms: constructive criticism and destructive criticism. Constructive criticism is meant to be helpful, while destructive criticism is meant to be offensive or shaming. People with low self-esteem tend to have difficulty hearing all forms of criticism and often respond in ways that are ineffective and ultimately reinforcing of low self-esteem.

When your self-esteem is low and you engage in your own negative self-talk, you become susceptible to believing and being hurt by the negative evaluations of others. Regardless of what they say, you take the criticism personally and allow it to serve as "proof" that you are not good enough. How you respond to criticism not only affects your self-esteem and the way you feel, but can also determine whether the situation escalates into an argument that can negatively impact relationships.

Regardless of the intent of the criticism, it will be helpful to pay close attention to how you react and to begin practicing more effective techniques for dealing with criticism. Responding to criticism in healthy ways can help protect as well as build your self-esteem. Let's first look at common ineffective responses to criticism and then look at healthier alternatives.

Ineffective Responses to Criticism[*]

In *Self-Esteem: A Proven Program of Cognitive Techniques for Assessing, Improving, & Maintaining Your Self-Esteem,* Matthew McKay, Ph.D., and Patrick Fanning discuss the following three ineffective ways that people tend to respond to criticism.

- **Aggressive Style:** You automatically respond to criticism by counterattacking, lashing out, and becoming defensive. Initially this approach may get people off your back; however, in the long run, it leads to the escalation of problems and to resentment, which can damage or destroy relationships. Because you are left feeling bad about yourself and guilty because of your aggressive reaction, self-esteem is further depleted.

   Example: "It's your fault I missed the turn. You were distracting me."

- **Passive Style:** Due to your own negative self-talk and distorted thinking, you immediately believe that any and all criticism of you is totally valid. Without stopping to consider whether the criticism is accurate and warranted, you automatically believe it is true.

   You agree with the criticism and surrender to the critic. You either apologize or remain silent. You may even join in the berating of your self-worth, either verbally or internally. Some critics will back down if you are silent and do not engage. While an apology or silence prevents you from having to come up with a protective response, you ultimately reinforce low self-esteem by not defending yourself and by potentially beating yourself up further.

   Another downside to the passive style is that your lack of self-esteem may be conveyed to the criticizer, which can leave you vulnerable to further attacks or to being taken advantage of because you are perceived to be in the weaker position.

   Example: "You're right. I'm sorry I missed the turn. I'm such an idiot."

---

[*] For more, see Matthew McKay, Ph.D., & Patrick Fanning's 2000 *Self-Esteem: A Proven Program of Cognitive Techniques for Assessing, Improving, & Maintaining Your Self-Esteem* (3rd ed.). Oakland, CA: New Harbinger Publications, Inc.

- **Passive-Aggressive Style:** You react with a combination of the two previous styles. Initially you apologize or agree with the criticism, but later you get even by some covertly aggressive act toward the critic. This is often unconscious and indirect. Self-esteem suffers twice; once when you agree with the criticism, and again when you retaliate. Again, this type of response can lead to resentment in relationships.

  Example: You are criticized by your partner for making a wrong turn on the way to dinner. You do not react to the criticism in the moment, but after dinner, you still feel affronted so you say you no longer want to go to the movie he/she was hoping to see.

These styles of responding to criticism are utilized before you even give yourself a chance to consider whether the criticism is valid and warranted. When self-esteem is low, you are unable to consider that somebody else's opinion or judgment may be wrong, unfair, or unwarranted, thus you surrender to their scrutiny without reflecting on your own opinion or analysis.

Effective Responses to Criticism[*]

As you work to build self-esteem, pay attention to your feelings and responses during times when you are criticized. Once you identify your pattern of responding you can work to replace ineffective methods with those that are more constructive. In *Self-Esteem: A Proven Program of Cognitive Techniques for Assessing, Improving, & Maintaining Your Self-Esteem*, Matthew McKay, Ph.D., and Patrick Fanning also offer the following suggested methods for more effectively dealing with criticism in ways that allow you to protect your self-esteem and prevent conflicts in relationships from escalating.

- **Acknowledgment:** If the criticism is accurate and valid, you can acknowledge it by agreeing. This tends to immediately stop further criticism. By acknowledging the criticism, you are agreeing that you made a mistake; however, you can still maintain your self-esteem by recognizing that making a mistake does not make you a bad or unworthy person.

  Acknowledgment only works to protect self-esteem if you truly agree with what the critic is saying. If you falsely agree, you deny yourself the ability to be assertive and have independent opinions, which works against building self-esteem.

---

[*] For more, see Matthew McKay, Ph.D., & Patrick Fanning's 2000 *Self-Esteem: A Proven Program of Cognitive Techniques for Assessing, Improving, & Maintaining Your Self-Esteem* (3rd ed.). Oakland, CA: New Harbinger Publications, Inc.

Four steps to acknowledgment are:

- Say "You're right."
- Paraphrase what the critic said to be sure you heard him/her correctly.
- Thank him/her if appropriate.
- Explain yourself, if appropriate, but remember that an explanation is not an apology. (People with low self-esteem tend to overapologize for mistakes.)

Example: "You're right. I missed the turn. I thought it was another block down, but I'm glad I know where it is now."

- **Clouding:** When you do not agree with or appreciate the criticism, you can use one of the following three clouding methods. These methods serve to quiet the critic without sacrificing your self-esteem.

  - **Agree in part:** Agree with just one part of what the critic is saying.

    Example:

    > Critic: "You missed the turn! We are going to be late. We will be the last people to get there!"

    > Response: "Yes, we will be late."

  - **Agree in probability:** Agree that there is a chance the criticism could be right, even if it's one in a million.

    Example:

    > Critic: "You missed the turn! We are going to be late. We will be the last people to get there!"

    > Response: "We could be the last to arrive."

  - **Agree in principle:** Acknowledge the critic's logic without endorsing all of his/her assumptions. Typically uses an "if/then" format.

Example:

> Critic: "You missed the turn! We are going to be late. We will be the last people to get there!"
>
> Response: "You're right. If we're late, we might be the last ones to get there."

- **Probing:** If you do not completely understand the criticism, you can use probing to clarify the intent and meaning behind the message. Probing means asking questions to find out more information about what the critic is actually intending. Once you have a better understanding, you can then decide whether the criticism is constructive and determine how you will respond—with acknowledgment or clouding. Key words to use include *exactly, specifically,* and *for example.*

  Examples:

  > "Exactly what do you mean by saying my performance was weak?"
  >
  > "Can you explain specifically what I did to upset you?"
  >
  > "Can you give me an example of what you would like me to help more with?"

  Oftentimes, the critic may simply be having a bad day, thus his/her remarks or tone come across the wrong way. By asking more questions you can clarify the situation and find out what is really going on. This is ultimately better for relationships and for your self-esteem than immediately taking a comment personally, becoming upset, and letting it impact your feelings of self-worth.

Healthy self-esteem means that you don't immediately accept all criticism at face value. Instead, you consider whether the criticism is accurate, invalid, or somewhere in between. Regardless of whether the criticism is warranted, when you stop to evaluate the message, you are protecting your self-esteem by sending yourself the message that your opinions, judgments, and beliefs are just as important as those of the critic.

As you work to build self-esteem, you may naturally begin responding differently to criticism, but it is also important to start paying attention to how criticism impacts you, since unhealthy responses to criticism can further deplete your self-esteem.

Additional Tips for Dealing with Criticisms

- Beware of the negative self-talk that may occur in response to criticism. Even if the criticism is accurate, remember that you are not a bad person for having faults or making mistakes. Everyone has weaknesses and mistakes are how we learn.

- Be careful of the tendency to get very defensive or angry in response to criticism. Take a step back before responding and avoid making excuses or lashing out. Instead, try to stay calm and collected when responding to critics. This rational, calm stance demonstrates healthy self-esteem, and establishing appropriate boundaries is something you can be proud of.

- All the composure and rationality in the world may not matter if you are dealing with an abusive or dysfunctional person. If the criticism is coming from a potentially abusive person or someone with a personality disorder (like narcissism, for example), it may be impossible to constructively deal with criticism. Instead, you will want to avoid getting into a power struggle and may need to walk away from the situation. Remember that an abusive person is the one with the problem, not you. Use healthy, rational self-talk to counter unwarranted criticism for yourself; for example, think to yourself something like, "I know I am a good person and I refuse to be brought down by the mean words of a bully."

- Sometimes it can be helpful to visualize something like an imaginary filter or shield in front of you when you are dealing with someone who is very negative or constantly critical. Imagine hurtful, mean, or unhelpful words getting stuck in the filter (just like dust particles in the air get trapped in the filter on a furnace) or being blocked by a shield so they cannot harm you. One client I worked with imagined her mother's critical comments rolling off her back the way water drops roll off the back of a duck. These visual images can help you to block the negativity of others from being internalized and damaging to your self-esteem.

Tips for Giving Criticism

It is often said that people with low self-esteem tend to tear others down in an unhealthy attempt to boost self-esteem and feel better about themselves. Bullies act tough and pick on others to hide their own feelings of unworthiness. Think about whether this has been true for you. Have you criticized or put others down as a result of your own poor self-esteem? If so, make a conscious effort to stop this behavior because hurting others only makes you feel worse about yourself at the end of the day. Remember that there is a difference between constructive criticism and destructive, shaming, and hurtful criticism. Constructive criticism can be necessary and worthwhile, while destructive criticism causes shame and hurt. Consider the following tips for delivering criticism to others:

- If appropriate, ask permission before giving your critique.

- Ensure that your message is constructive and purposeful rather than meant to embarrass, hurt, or belittle the other person.

- Avoid delivering criticism when you are angry, irritable, or defensive. Instead, wait until you are calm and rational.

- Be specific about your message, offering examples or alternatives.

- Be careful not to use all-or-nothing language, including words like *always* and *never.*

- Avoid labels and name-calling.

- Avoid mocking, blaming, and preaching.

Compliments

The flip side to a criticism is a compliment, and how you respond to praise is also an important part of self-esteem. It might seem that when your self-esteem is low, you crave compliments in order to build yourself up; however, external validation is not enough to build self-esteem. Although people with low self-esteem may want compliments, they tend to have a difficult time hearing and accepting them. Positive feedback tends to be filtered or interrupted by negative self-talk, which instead interjects with negative messages. Minimization and mind reading are common. For example, you rebuff compliments by telling yourself things like, "He is lying. You didn't do that well," or, "She's just saying that to be nice; she doesn't really mean it."

As you are working to build self-esteem, pay attention to the compliments and positive feedback you receive from others. Monitor both your external and internal reactions and notice when negative self-talk occurs in an attempt to block a compliment. You may be surprised at how many compliments you downplay or completely miss. Use the thought-stopping and thought-replacing tools to catch any distorted thinking that tries to oppose or block compliments. Instead, allow yourself to accept the compliment gracefully by thanking the person complimenting you. Start with smaller compliments, such as, "Nice shirt," and build your way up to being able to accept and believe compliments that are directly about you. When responding to a compliment, the only response necessary is a simple "Thank you."

Giving Compliments

You can also practice giving compliments to others. Giving compliments often makes us feel good about ourselves. When you give a compliment, pay attention to how others react and consider the differences between times when your compliments are accepted and acknowledged with gratitude, versus times when they are minimized or rejected. You may notice that it doesn't feel very good to have somebody dismiss a compliment. Recognizing this may help you to improve your own reactions to receiving compliments.

Recommended Journaling

Criticisms & Compliments

Criticisms:

Think about how you react to criticism from others. When do you find it difficult to hear criticism? Are there certain areas where criticism feels especially bad? Do you tend to respond to criticism with a passive or aggressive response? Do you ever use the passive-aggressive response method? Do you respond one way in certain situations and another way in others? How do you think your responses to criticism affect your self-esteem? Your relationships with others?

What would you like to change regarding receiving criticism? Consider how you respond to criticism from various people—your family, your friends, your boss, your co-workers/classmates, acquaintances, strangers. What do you think influences the way you react to criticism?

How are you with *giving* criticism? Is it difficult for you to give criticism to others? Do any of your roles make it necessary to critique others? If so, how do they tend to respond? Are there certain situations when it is more difficult to give criticism and are there certain people with whom it is more difficult to give criticism? Do you ever find that your criticism is not as effective as you would like? What could help to make your criticism more effective?

Compliments:

Think about how you react to compliments from others. Are you able to receive compliments from others gracefully or do you habitually dismiss or deny their legitimacy? How do you think your responses affect your self-esteem and your relationships?

Keep a list of compliments you receive from others this week. Pay attention to what your reactions to these compliments are. Do you doubt if you deserve the praise and recognition? Do you tend to minimize or reject certain compliments? Does negative self-talk creep in when you are paid a compliment? Does negative self-talk work to convince you that you are not really worthy or deserving of praise?

Pay attention to what happens when you compliment others. Consider what others' reactions are to praise. Think about how various responses (and possible alternative responses) to compliments may affect the person giving the compliment, the relationship, and your own self-esteem.

10

Assertiveness

Questions to Consider

- What is assertiveness?

- What are the advantages and disadvantages of being assertive?

- Consider where you currently are with assertiveness. Are you able to stand up for yourself? Are you able to ask for what you want or need? Are you able to voice your opinions?

- When is it harder to be assertive and when is it easier?

- Are there certain groups of people you are able to assert yourself with and others you are not?

- Is there anything you would like to change about your current ability to be assertive?

- What are the differences between assertiveness and passivity? Between assertiveness and aggression?

- How do you think assertiveness affects self-esteem?

The Assertiveness Inventory[*]

The following inventory is from *Your Perfect Right: Assertiveness and Equality in Your Life and Relationships* (9th edition), by Robert E. Alberti and Michael L. Emmons. It can help you get an idea of where you stand regarding assertiveness today. Paying attention to difficulties in assertiveness and learning to act more assertively in various situations help to build self-esteem.

Be honest in your responses. All you have to do is draw a circle around the number that describes you best. For some questions, the assertive end of the scale is at 0, for others at 3.

0 = No or Never
1 = Somewhat or Sometimes
2 = Usually or A Good Deal
3 = Practically Always or Entirely

1.)   When a person is highly unfair, do you call it to attention?   0 1 2 3

2.)   Do you find it difficult to make decisions?   0 1 2 3

3.)   Are you openly critical of others' ideas, opinions, behavior?   0 1 2 3

4.)   Do you speak out in protest when someone takes your place in line?   0 1 2 3

5.)   Do you often avoid people or situations for fear of embarrassment?   0 1 2 3

6.)   Do you usually have confidence in your own judgment?   0 1 2 3

7.)   Do you insist that your spouse or roommate take on a fair share of household chores?   0 1 2 3

8.)   Are you prone to "fly off the handle?"   0 1 2 3

9.)   When a salesperson makes an effort, do you find it hard to say no even though the merchandise is not really what you want?   0 1 2 3

10.) When a latecomer is waited on before you are, do you call attention to the situation?   0 1 2 3

11.) Are you reluctant to speak up in a discussion or debate?   0 1 2 3

12.) If a person has borrowed money (or a book, garment, thing of value) and is overdue in returning it, do you mention it?   0 1 2 3

13.) Do you continue to pursue an argument after the other person has had enough?   0 1 2 3

14.) Do you generally express what you feel?   0 1 2 3

15.) Are you disturbed if someone watches you at work?   0 1 2 3

16.) If someone keeps kicking or bumping your chair in a movie or a lecture, do you ask the person to stop?   0 1 2 3

17.) Do you find it difficult to keep eye contact when talking to another person?   0 1 2 3

18.) In a good restaurant when your meal is improperly prepared or served, do you ask the waitperson to correct the situation?   0 1 2 3

19.) When you discover merchandise is faulty, do you return it for an adjustment?   0 1 2 3

20.) Do you show your anger by name-calling or obscenities?   0 1 2 3

21.) Do you try to be a wallflower or a piece of the furniture in social situations?   0 1 2 3

22.) Do you insist that your property manager (mechanic, repairman, etc.) make repairs, adjustments, or replacements which are his/her responsibility?   0 1 2 3

23.) Do you often step in and make decisions for others?   0 1 2 3

24.) Are you able to express love and affection openly?   0 1 2 3

25.) Are you able to ask your friends for small favors or help?   0 1 2 3

26.) Do you think you always have the right answer? 0 1 2 3

27.) When you differ with a person you respect, are you able to speak up for your own viewpoint? 0 1 2 3

28.) Are you able to refuse unreasonable requests friends make? 0 1 2 3

29.) Do you have difficulty complimenting or praising others? 0 1 2 3

30.) If someone smoking nearby disturbs you, can you say so? 0 1 2 3

31.) Do you shout or use bullying tactics to get others to do as you wish? 0 1 2 3

32.) Do you finish other people's sentences for them? 0 1 2 3

33.) Do you get into physical fights with others, especially with strangers? 0 1 2 3

34.) At family meals, do you control the conversation? 0 1 2 3

35.) When you meet a stranger, are you the first to introduce yourself and begin a conversation? 0 1 2 3

Analyzing Your Results

Look at individual events in your life involving particular people or groups and consider your strengths and shortcomings accordingly.

Look at your responses to questions 1, 2, 4, 5, 6, 7, 9, 10, 11, 12, 14, 15, 16, 17, 18, 19, 21, 22, 24, 25, 27, 28, 30, and 35. These questions are oriented toward nonassertive behavior. Do your answers to these items tell you that you are rarely speaking up for yourself? Or are there perhaps some specific situations that give you trouble?

Look at your responses to questions 3, 8, 13, 20, 23, 26, 29, 31, 32, 33, and 34. These questions are oriented toward aggressive behavior. Do your answers to these questions suggest you are pushing others around more than you realized?

Assertiveness

One consequence of low self-esteem is the inability to stand up for yourself or ask for what you want. You may have a hard time handling various situations that require making a request, asking for help, stating an opinion, pointing out a problem, expressing feelings, or asking questions. This inability to speak up can leave you feeling taken advantage of and being the victim of unfair circumstances. For example, when you have a hard time being assertive, you may be unable to speak up if somebody charges you the wrong amount, does an unsatisfactory job on a project you've hired him/her for, or stands you up. Additionally, you may find it too difficult to ask questions in a meeting or class, ask for a favor, or make a request regarding something you desire or need. Everyday tasks, like returning an item to the store, ordering food at a restaurant, and talking on the phone can be a challenge.

The inability to be assertive often coincides with low self-esteem because people with low self-esteem are often unaware of their own needs or afraid their needs are not important. They may feel unworthy or may be too insecure and anxious to speak up and voice their own opinions. This reluctance to speak up is reinforced by irrational beliefs and negative self-talk that convince you that speaking up will result in embarrassment, rejection, or failure. The longer you spend avoiding being assertive, the more reinforced low self-esteem becomes. Learning and practicing assertiveness skills can help you to develop self-respect and self-worth, which ultimately help you to build self-esteem.

In *Your Perfect Right: Assertiveness and Equality in Your Life and Relationships* (9th edition), Robert Alberti, Ph.D., and Michael Emmons, Ph.D., provide the following definition of healthy assertive communication:

> Assertive self-expression is direct, firm, positive—and when necessary persistent—action intended to promote equality in person-to-person relationships. Assertiveness enables us to act in our own best interests, to stand up for ourselves without undue anxiety, to exercise personal rights without denying the rights of others, and to express our feelings (e.g. affection, love, friendship, disappointment, annoyance, anger, regret, sorrow) honestly and comfortably.[*]

Assertiveness includes the ability to initiate and engage in conversations and to express opinions, thoughts, and feelings, both positive and negative. It allows you to clearly express your needs and desires, give compliments and

---

[*] Copyright © 2008 by Robert Alberti, Ph.D. & Michael Emmons, Ph.D., from *Your Perfect Right: Assertiveness and Equality in Your Life and Relationships* (9th ed.). Atascadero, CA: Impact Publishers. Reprinted by permission of Impact Publishers.

criticisms, and make or refuse requests. Assertiveness also allows you to stand up for yourself, defend you rights, and set limits and boundaries with others. Some examples of assertive messages include the following:

Messages that convey feelings or opinions:

- I am angry that you lied to me.
- I am unhappy with this plan.
- I am disappointed in your behavior.
- I believe you have treated me unfairly.
- I do not agree with you.

Messages that express desires or set limits and boundaries:

- No.
- I am unavailable to help.
- I would rather not participate.
- I am next in line.
- I want to handle this myself.

When you learn to speak up for yourself, you become more confident and are better able to protect yourself. This sense of self-expression and self-protection helps to maintain self-esteem. As you become more assertive, you'll find that you like yourself better and are better able to enforce healthy boundaries. With practice, you may find that you gain equality in relationships and that others will begin responding to you in more satisfying ways.

Of course there will be some situations where others will not embrace your assertiveness. There are always going to be those difficult people and those challenging situations where it seems that no matter what you say or how you say it, certain people do not hear or respect you. Sometimes, you may not be able to accomplish your end goal; however, in these instances, acting assertively is still important as a means to protect self-esteem. For example, your assertive message may seem to fall on deaf ears or you may not get the reaction you hoped for; however, the fact that you spoke up sends the message that you value your own opinion and acknowledge your right to say what is on your mind. This message helps you to maintain self-esteem and also demonstrates the boundary that you will not shirk away from conflict or allow yourself to be taken advantage of.

When you act assertively and are met with resistance or invalidation from others, it's what you do with that invalidation that affects self-esteem. Beating yourself up with self-talk messages that say "You should have kept your mouth shut. You made a fool out of yourself and now he thinks you are ridiculous" will hurt your self-esteem, while healthy messages, such as "He may not have liked what I had to say but I'm proud of myself for acting assertively" will maintain self-esteem.

Remember that negative or discouraging responses from others are not necessarily about anything you said or did wrong. Instead, they are often about insecurities, weaknesses, faults, or differing opinions in the other person. As with developing better boundaries, expect that you will initially be met with resistance from others as you practice assertiveness. Change is difficult for most people and the individuals in your life will have to make their own adjustments to adapt to your new assertive ways. If you are dealing with an abusive or narcissistic person, you may have to pick your battles and anticipate that assertiveness will be harder. Rational self-talk can help you to remember, "His negative reaction is about him, not about anything wrong with me."

Assertiveness: A Skill You Can Learn

The good news about assertiveness is that it is not necessarily an inborn trait. Rather, it is a skill that can be learned. In the past, you may have witnessed and envied others who seem to have the confidence to speak up and you may have wished you could be more like this. The reality is, you can become more assertive with practice. Assertiveness is something that can be taught, practiced, and improved upon. Doing so will help to build your self-esteem.

In *Asserting Yourself: A Practical Guide for Positive Change,* Sharon Anthony Bower and Gordon H. Bower state the following things that assertive people are able to do:[*]

- **Use feeling talk:** You can express your personal likes and interests spontaneously rather than stating things in neutral terms. You say, "I like this soup" or "I love your blouse" rather than, "This soup is good." You can use the phrases "I feel" or "I think" when it's appropriate.

- **Talk about yourself:** If you do something worthwhile and interesting, you can let your friends know about it. You don't monopolize the conversation, but you can mention your accomplishments when it is appropriate.

- **Make greeting-talk:** You are outgoing and friendly with people you want to know better. You smile brightly and sound pleased to see them. You say, "Well, hello! How good to see you again" rather than softly mumbling "H'lo" or nodding silently or looking embarrassed.

---

[*] From *Asserting Yourself: A Practical Guide for Positive Change,* by Sharon Anthony Bower and Gordon H. Bower, Copyright © 1991. Reprinted by permission of Da Capo Press, a member of The Perseus Books Group.

- **Accept compliments:** You can accept compliments graciously ("Yes, I like this shirt, too") rather than disagreeing with them ("Oh, this old thing?"). You reward rather than punish your complimenter.

- **Use appropriate facial talk:** Your facial expressions and voice inflections convey the same feelings your words are conveying. You can look people directly in the eye when conversing with them.

- **Disagree mildly:** When you disagree with someone, you do not pretend to agree for the sake of keeping the peace. You can convey your disagreement mildly by looking away, or grimacing, or raising eyebrows, or shaking your head, or changing the topic of conversation.

- **Ask for clarification:** If someone gives you garbled directions, instructions, or explanations, you can ask that person to restate them more clearly. Rather than going away confused and feeling dumb, you can say, "Your directions were not clear to me. Would you please go over them again?"

- **Ask why:** When you are asked to do something that does not seem reasonable or enjoyable, you can ask, "Why do you want me to do that?"

- **Express active disagreement:** When you disagree with someone and feel sure of your ground, you can express your disagreement by saying things like, "I have a different view of that matter. My opinion is…" or "I think your opinion leaves out of consideration the following factors…"

- **Speak up for your rights:** You do not let others take advantage of you when you feel put upon; you can say no persistently without feeling guilty. You can demand your rights and ask to be treated with fairness and justice. You can say, "I was next in line," or "Excuse me, but you will have to leave as I have another appointment now," or "Please turn down your radio," or "You're half an hour late for our appointment." You can register your complaints firmly without blowing up.

- **Be persistent:** If you have a legitimate complaint, you can continue to restate it, despite resistance from the other party, until you get satisfaction. You do not allow one or two no's to cause you to give up.

- **Avoid justifying every opinion:** In discussion, if someone continually argues and asks you "why, why, why," you can stop the questioning by refusing to go along, or by reflecting it back to the other person. You can state simply, "That's just the way I feel. Those are my values. I don't have to justify everything I say. If justifying is so important to you, you might try justifying why you're disagreeing with me so much."

What Assertiveness Is and Is Not

Assertiveness does not mean manipulating, controlling, or demeaning others. Instead, assertiveness is about expressing yourself in a manner that is direct and self-assured, yet respectful of others. Assertiveness includes standing up for yourself; expressing your feelings, ideas, and opinions; asking for what you want; and saying no to things you don't want. Assertiveness includes communication that is neither passive and submissive nor aggressive.

When you do not act assertively, you become dependent on others to make decisions for you, which makes it even harder to be aware of your own needs and desires. You tend to conform to the desires and expectations of others, losing yourself in the process. Once you fall into a pattern of being nonassertive, it becomes even harder to act assertively, because you may fear creating conflict or "rocking the boat." When you habitually avoid speaking up or being assertive, you risk losing the ability to protect yourself when assertiveness really is necessary, such as in situations where you are in danger of being hurt, abused, or taken advantage of. Though challenging, learning to be more assertive is a way to build and demonstrate self-esteem.

Assertiveness is often confused with aggressive behavior and some people are afraid that acting more assertively will make them appear rude or egotistical; however, assertion and aggression are not the same. While aggression involves hostile and attacking words and behaviors that put other people down, assertion uses neutral wording and a calm demeanor to deliver messages. Assertion does not involve hurting the other person physically or emotionally. You can stand up for yourself in a manner that is also respectful of the other person. While it is okay to be angry and to express anger, it is not okay to belittle, hurt, or attack another person. By learning the differences between assertiveness and aggression, you can ensure that your messages convey your emotions without crossing the line toward aggressiveness.

Nonassertion vs. Aggression vs. Assertion

In *Your Perfect Right: Assertiveness and Equality in Your Life and Relationships* (9th edition), Robert Alberti, Ph.D., and Michael Emmons, Ph.D., provide the following chart that highlights the differences among nonassertive, aggressive, and assertive behaviors:

Nonassertive	Aggressive	Assertive[*]
Sender	Sender	Sender
Self-denying	Self-enhancing at expense of others	Self-enhancing
Inhibited	Expressive	Expressive
Hurt, anxious	Controlling	Feels good about self
Allows others to choose	Chooses for others	Chooses for self
Does not achieve desired goals	Achieves desired goals by hurting others	May achieve desired goals
Receiver	Receiver	Receiver
Guilty or angry	Self-denying	Self-enhancing
Depreciates sender	Hurt, defensive, humiliated	Expressive
Achieves desired goals at sender's expense	Does not achieve desired goals	May achieve desired goals

Forming Assertive Messages

As you begin practicing assertiveness, it may be helpful to start by writing examples of assertive messages, requests, and responses down on paper. This will help you to formulate the messages into sentences and give you the opportunity to ensure your word choices are neither passive nor aggressive. Consider overall situations where you could use more assertiveness, or think of specific times you wish you had acted more assertively, and work on preparing examples of assertive messages for these scenarios. Keep in mind the following qualities of assertive behavior, which appear in *Your Perfect Right:*

Eleven Key Points About Assertive Behavior:[*]

- *Self-expressive*
- *Respectful* of the rights of others
- *Honest*
- *Direct and firm*
- *Equalizing*, benefiting both parties in a relationship
- Both *verbal* (including the content of the message) and *nonverbal* (including the style of the message)
- *Positive* at times (expressing affection, praise, appreciation) and *negative* at times (expressing limits, anger, criticism)
- *Appropriate for the person and situation,* not universal
- *Socially responsible*
- *Learned,* not inborn
- As *persistent* as is necessary to achieve one's goals without violating the ten points above

Formulas for Assertive Messages

When formulating an assertive message, consider your main goal. Is there something you want or need? Or is there a feeling you need to express? Think about how you can articulate your message in a calm, concise manner. Some experts in assertiveness training suggest using various formulas when attempting to create assertive messages. While a formula will not always fit the specific situation or be readily accessible, utilizing these blueprints to practice can be helpful. Some suggested formulas and examples follow:

---

[*] Copyright © 2008 by Robert Alberti, Ph.D., & Michael Emmons, Ph.D., from *Your Perfect Right: Assertiveness and Equality in Your Life and Relationships* (9th ed.). Atascadero, CA: Impact Publishers. Reprinted by permission of Impact Publishers.

Formula 1:

When you need to make a request, consider the details of what you want, from whom, when, and where, then formulate these items into a statement that is direct and specific. (The order can be switched around as necessary for your statement.)

What I want: _____

From whom: _____

When: _____

Where: _____

Example:

> **What I want:** Help with cleaning
> **Who:** Kids
> **When:** Saturday, before playing with friends
> **Where:** Garage

Assertive message: "I want you and your brother to help me clean out the garage this Saturday morning before you play with your friends."

Formula 2:

When you need to express your feelings about a situation, consider the specific emotion, what caused it, and what you would like to be different:

I feel: _____

When you: _____

I want you to: _____

Example:

Feeling: Hurt, upset, irritated

When: My husband ignores me when I am telling him about my day

Want: Husband to pay attention

Assertive message: "I feel very hurt and irritated when you ignore me when I am telling you about my day. I would like you to put down your book and make eye contact when I am speaking to you."

DESC Scripts[*]

In *Asserting Yourself: A Practical Guide for Positive Change,* Sharon Anthony Bower and Gordon H. Bower describe a four-step program called DESC, which helps individuals to write successful scripts for delivering assertive messages. These scripts can be useful when addressing someone who has done something to upset you. DESC stands for Describe, Express, Specify, and Consequences. The idea behind DESC scripts is to ask yourself the following questions as you prepare your message:

- What unwanted behavior has been displayed? (Describe)

- How can I express the way I feel about this behavior? (Express)

- What behavioral changes might I contract for? Also, what might I need to change in my behavior? (Specify)

- What rewarding consequences can I provide for sticking to the contract? (Consequences)

The Bowers provide the following rules for preparing assertive DESC scripts:

Rules for Assertive DESC Scripts[*]

Describe

Do	Don't
Describe the other person's behavior objectively.	Describe your emotional reaction to it.
Use concrete terms.	Use abstract, vague terms.
Describe a specified time, place, and frequency of the action.	Generalize for "all time."
Describe the action, not the "motive."	Guess at the other person's motives or goals.

Express

Do	Don't
Express your feelings.	Deny your feelings.
Express them calmly.	Unleash emotional outburst.
State feelings in a positive manner, as relating to a goal to be achieved.	State feelings negatively, making put-down or attack.
Direct yourself to the specific offending behavior, not to the whole person.	Attack the entire character of the person.

---

[*] From *Asserting Yourself: A Practical Guide for Positive Change* by Sharon Anthony Bower and Gordon H. Bower, Copyright © 1991. Reprinted by permission of Da Capo Press, a member of The Perseus Books Group.

Specify

Do	Don't
Ask explicitly for change in the other person's behavior.	Merely imply that you'd like a change.
Request a small change.	Ask for too large a change.
Request only one or two changes at one time.	Ask for too many changes.
Specify the concrete actions you want to see stopped, and those you want to see performed.	Ask for changes in nebulous traits or qualities.
Take account of whether the other person can meet your request without suffering large losses.	Ignore the other person's needs or ask only for your satisfaction.
Specify (if appropriate) what behavior you are willing to change to make the agreement.	Consider that only the other person has to change.

Consequences

Do	Don't
Make the consequences explicit.	Be ashamed to talk about rewards and penalties.
Give a positive reward for change in the desired direction.	Give only punishments for lack of change.
Select something that is desirable and reinforcing to the other person.	Select something that only you might find rewarding.

Select a reward that is big enough to maintain the behavior change.	Offer a reward you can't or won't deliver.
Select a punishment of a magnitude that "fits the crime" or refusing to change behavior.	Make exaggerated threats.
Select a punishment that you are actually willing to carry out.	Use unrealistic threats or self-defeating punishments.

Delivering Assertive Messages

When you are delivering an assertive message it is important to pay attention not only to the content and words of the message, but also to the tone of your voice and to your nonverbal behaviors. Try to remain calm and confident, and avoid showing fear or nervousness. A message comes across much more assertively when you speak clearly and audibly, use good eye contact, and maintain an open and confident body posture. If you slouch, look at the floor, apologize, mumble, or speak too softly, you will not be taken seriously or your words will be lost. Further, your lack of self-esteem will be apparent and the interaction likely will not go over well, reinforcing low self-esteem and feelings of unworthiness.

Also, remember to be specific about what you are saying or asking, providing examples when necessary. If you are making a request, keep it small and do not ask for too many things at once. Keeping your message simple and concise will make it easier for the recipient to truly hear what you are saying. Be sure that you make requests rather than demands or ultimatums. Also, take care not to whine or nag. If you are expressing frustration with someone, be sure your comments are constructive rather than shaming or ridiculing. Focus on behaviors the other person has control over, rather than on personal attacks about his/her character.

When delivering an assertive message, it is also important to be mindful of the location and timing. Sometimes messages are best received when they are given right away after an incident. However, if you are very angry or upset, it will be in your best interest to take some time to cool off, gather your thoughts, and think through your wording before responding. There is nothing wrong with revisiting a topic in a constructive way later; for example, by saying something like, "I have been thinking about something you said earlier and wanted to get a few things off my chest," or "After processing some of my feelings, I wanted to let you know some of my thoughts."

Some situations warrant selecting a more appropriate time or location to deliver your assertive message; for example, if you need to assert yourself with your boss, it may be more appropriate to do so later and in private, rather than immediately and in front of other co-workers. By ensuring the most appropriate timing and location for delivering your message, you take care not to shame or embarrass the other person.

Other Assertiveness Tips & Techniques

Different situations call for different types of assertiveness and will require different techniques depending on the circumstances and audience you are speaking to. The following methods may be useful in delivering assertive messages:

- **Time-Out:**

   Sometimes it may be necessary and useful to use a time-out. If you are uncertain what you want or how you should best phrase your message, you can ask for a time-out by saying something like, "I need to think about this. Let's talk more later," or "I need to process my feelings. Let me get back to you when I'm ready to talk more." This technique is also useful if you are very upset or angry, as it provides you with some time to cool off. This helps make it easier to deliver your message assertively rather than aggressively.

   Examples: "I need to think about this and get more information before I can give my opinion. Let me get back to you this afternoon." Or "Let me get a cup of coffee and we'll talk again in an hour."

- **Defusing / Deescalating:**

   Defusing or deescalating can be used when the other person is very angry or aggressive. It's a way to calm things down rather than engage in the intensity, allowing the situation to escalate. To defuse, you acknowledge what the person is saying but agree to continue the conversation only once the person has calmed down.

   Example: "I see that you are very upset. I want to talk about this more but think we should wait until we are both in a calmer place. Let's each go think about what it is we need to communicate and then revisit the conversation in an hour or so."

- **Fogging:**

  Fogging can be used in responding to a person who has criticized you. By fogging, you neither agree nor disagree with the criticism, you simply acknowledge it and move on.

  Example: "I understand you think I'm being too strict, but I have not changed my mind about letting you go to the party."

- **Broken Record:**

  This is a useful technique when somebody is trying to argue, dismiss, or ignore your message. It allows you to keep repeating your message until you are heard. By using the broken record method, you listen respectfully to the other person but avoid engaging in any points that contradict or dismiss your message. Instead, you keep repeating your message until it is heard.

  Examples: "I agree, but unfortunately, I am not available to help with this project." Or, "Thank you for the information but I am still not interested." You may need to continue repeating the phrase or message several times.

- **Mirroring:**

  Asking the other person to mirror or repeat back what you have said can be useful when you do not think he/she is listening or understanding what you are saying. If the person is unable to capture your main points when repeating back what you have said, it gives you the opportunity to clarify your message.

  Example: "I'm not sure I'm making my point clear. Can you tell me what you've heard me say?"

- **"No" Sandwich:**

  Sandwiching an assertive message between two positive (or neutral) statements can help to soften the message and create a better chance that the other person will listen and hear your message without becoming immediately offended or defensive. This can be especially helpful when your message is about setting limits or turning someone down.

Example: "I really appreciate that you think I would be a good volunteer for the fundraiser. Unfortunately, I cannot commit this year but hope I will have more time to help next year."

- **Preface with a Disclaimer:**

  When you anticipate that your message will offend the other person or will make him/her defensive before you have even finished speaking, it may be useful to preface your message with a sentence that acknowledges this.

  Example: "I know you are not going to be happy with what I have to say, but I'd like you to hear me out. I've decided not to accept the job and my reasons are the following…" Or "I don't want you to think I don't want to see you; however, my schedule is already very busy so I'm unable to make plans at the moment."

- **I Statements:**

  When communicating with others, it is often useful to speak from a first-person perspective and use *I* statements rather than *you* statements. Statements that begin with *you* have the potential to come across as personal attacks, which sets the receiver up for defensiveness. This detracts from his/her ability to really hear your message. By formatting your statement to begin with an *I* message, you have a better chance of delivering a message that comes across as assertive rather than aggressive.

  Example: "*I* was very disappointed that you did not do the chores I asked you to do last night" versus "*You* didn't do the chores I asked you to do!" Or, "*I* would appreciate it if you could take out the trash" instead of "*You* need to take out the trash."

Dealing with Resistance to Your Assertions

Regardless of how well formulated and effective your message and delivery may be, there will always be times when you are confronted with difficult people who challenge your messages. In *Asserting Yourself: A Practical Guide for Positive Change,* Sharon Anthony Bower and Gordon H. Bower give examples of effective counter-reply methods that can be used when someone tries to ignore, argue with, or avoid listening to your assertive message. They are as follows:[*]

- **Persist:** (Similar to the broken record technique) Repeat your main point, the object of your assertion (usually this is your Specify line in a DESC script).

- **Disagree:** Make a straightforward, direct statement. ("I don't agree.")

- **Emphasize feelings/thoughts:** Stress your feelings or thoughts about the behavior or situation, giving more details or calling attention to their importance. ("This is important to me.")

- **Agree...But:** Agree with the other person's right to have certain feelings and draw certain conclusions, but disagree with the idea that you must hold the same feelings or draw the same conclusions.

- **Dismiss:** Ignore the detouring comment completely or—better—quickly deny its relevance to the problem under discussion. ("That's not the point here.")

- **Redefine:** Don't accept someone's negative label for your behavior; redefine your behavior in positive terms. ("I'm not being nosy; I'm just being naturally curious about a friend.")

- **Answer quickly:** Sometimes it's best to answer with a simple yes or no or with some other brief, direct reply, so you can get on with your central concern.

- **Ask a question:** Instead of accepting vague criticism, ask for clarification. ("In what ways do you think I'm acting foolishly?")

- **Stipulate consequences:** When pushed to the limit of your tolerance or where you feel threatened, consider promising realistic, negative consequences if the offensive behavior continues. (Beware of this approach, because it may backfire.)

Irrational Beliefs & Assertiveness

As you are practicing assertiveness, pay attention to your irrational beliefs as they relate to assertiveness. Just as irrational beliefs keep you trapped in a

---

[*] From *Asserting Yourself: A Practical Guide for Positive Change* by Sharon Anthony Bower and Gordon H. Bower, Copyright © 1991. Reprinted by permission of Da Capo Press, a member of The Perseus Books Group.

place of low self-esteem, they also make it difficult to act assertively. Irrational thinking often tells us that our own thoughts are not important or worthwhile. Additionally, anxious and negative self-talk makes us fearful of judgment and rejection. We wind up convincing ourselves that our own ideas are stupid or that we might appear foolish or wrong if we voice an opinion or ask a question. We become reluctant to speak up and wind up reinforcing low self-esteem.

In *The New Assertive Woman: Be Your Own Person Through Assertive Training,* Lynn Z. Bloom, Karen Coburn, and Joan Pearlman provide the following examples of common irrational beliefs regarding assertiveness, as well as their rational counterparts. Once we recognize our irrational beliefs about assertiveness, we can work toward incorporating more rational ideas into our thinking, which will ultimately allow us to begin acting more assertively. As you read over the list, consider whether you identify with any of these irrational beliefs. If so, make an effort to dispute them so you are ultimately able to practice assertiveness.

Irrational Beliefs Regarding Assertiveness[*]

1. **If I assert myself, others will get mad at me.**

   Rational counterparts: If I assert myself, the effects may be positive, neutral, or negative. However, since assertion involves legitimate rights, I feel that the odds are in my favor to have some positive result. If I assert myself people may or may not get mad at me/they may feel closer to me/like what I say or do/help me to solve the problem.

2. **If I assert myself and people do become angry with me, I will be devastated: It will be awful.**

   Rational counterparts: Even if others do become angry and unpleasant, I am capable of handling it without falling apart. If I assert myself when it is appropriate, I don't have to feel responsible for the other person's anger. It may be his problem.

3. **Although I prefer others to be straightforward with me, I am afraid that if I am open with others and say "no," I will hurt them.**

Rational counterparts: If I am assertive, other people may or may not feel hurt. Most people are not more fragile than I am. If I prefer to be dealt with directly, quite likely others will too.

4. ***If my assertion hurts others, I am responsible for their feelings.***

   Rational counterparts: Even if others do feel hurt by my assertive behavior, I can let them know I care for them while also being direct about what I need or want. Although at times others will be taken aback by my assertive behavior, most people are not so vulnerable and fragile that they will be shattered by it.

5. ***It is wrong and selfish to turn down legitimate requests. Other people will think I'm terrible and won't like me.***

   Rational counterparts: Even legitimate requests can be refused assertively. It is acceptable to consider my own needs—sometimes before those of others. I can't please all of the people all of the time.

6. ***At all costs, I must avoid making statements and asking questions that might make me look ignorant or stupid.***

   Rational counterparts: It's all right to lack information or to make a mistake. It just shows I am human.

7. ***Assertive women are cold, castrating bitches. If I'm assertive, I'll be so unpleasant that people won't like me.***

   Rational counterpart: Assertive women are direct and honest, and they behave appropriately. They show a genuine concern for other people's rights and feelings, while demonstrating self-respect by also caring about their own rights and feelings. Their assertiveness enriches their relationships with others.

Affirming Assertiveness

As you work on disputing irrational thoughts related to assertiveness, begin to consider what your personal thoughts, feelings, opinions, wants, and needs are. Work on adding statements that foster assertiveness and a right to speak up for yourself into your list of affirmations.

The following list of personal rights appears in *The Anxiety and Phobia Workbook* (4th edition) by Edmund J. Bourne, Ph.D. The list of basic tenets of an assertive philosophy on the following page are by Patricia Jakubowski in *Psychotherapy for Women: Treatment Toward Equality,* edited by Edna I. Rawlings and Dianne K. Carter. These lists tend to be extremely useful for people with low self-esteem who have difficulty believing they inherently have rights that allow them to stand up for themselves or be assertive. Reading these lists on a regular basis will help you to form a foundation of healthy self-esteem and an attitude that allows you to be assertive.

When you first read over the lists, pay attention to any points that seem untrue or foreign to you. These points are things you will want to work into your daily affirmations. The more you read over these lists and repeat the affirmative statements, the more you will begin to believe these rights and behaviors are truly yours. Remember that repetition rewires the brain. Repeating the rights from these lists on a regular basis will help to shift your beliefs toward those that foster the ability to be assertive.

My Personal Bill of Rights[*]

- I have the right to ask for what I want.

- I have the right to say no to requests or demands I can't meet.

- I have the right to express all of my feelings, positive or negative.

- I have the right to change my mind.

- I have the right to make mistakes and not have to be perfect.

- I have the right to follow my own values and standards.

- I have the right to say no to anything when I feel I am not ready, it is unsafe, or it violates my values.

- I have the right to determine my own priorities.

- I have the right *not* to be responsible for others' behavior, actions, feelings, or problems.

- I have the right to expect honesty from others.

- I have the right to be angry at someone I love.

- I have the right to be uniquely myself.

- I have the right to feel scared and say, "I'm scared."

- I have the right to say, "I don't know."

- I have the right not to give excuses or reasons for my behavior.

- I have the right to make decisions based on my feelings.

- I have the right to my own needs for personal space and time.

- I have the right to be playful and frivolous.

- I have the right to be healthier than those around me.

- I have the right to be in a non-abusive environment.

- I have the right to make friends and be comfortable around people.

- I have the right to change and grow.

- I have the right to have my needs and wants respected by others.

- I have the right to be treated with dignity and respect.

- I have the right to be happy.

The Basic Tenets of an Assertive Philosophy[*]

- By standing up for our rights we show we respect ourselves and achieve respect from other people.

- By trying to govern our lives so as to never hurt anyone, we end up hurting ourselves and other people.

- Sacrificing our rights usually results in destroying relationships or preventing new ones from forming.

- Not letting others know how we feel and what we think is a form of selfishness.

- Sacrificing our rights usually results in training other people to mistreat us.

- If we don't tell other people how their behavior negatively affects us, we are denying them an opportunity to change their behavior.

- We can decide what's important for us; we do not have to suffer from the *tyranny of the should and should not.*

- When we do what we think is right for us, we feel better about ourselves and have more authentic and satisfying relationships with others.

- We all have a natural right to courtesy and respect.

- We all have a right to express ourselves as long as we don't violate the rights of others.

- There is more to be gained from life by being free and able to stand up for ourselves and from honoring the same rights of other people.

- When we are assertive everyone involved usually benefits.

---

[*] Copyright © 1977 by Patricia Jakubowski. Self-Assertion Training Procedures for Women. In D. Carter and E. Rawlings (Eds). *Psychotherapy for Women: Treatment Toward Equality* (pp. 168-190). Springfield, IL: Charles C. Thomas Publishers, Ltd. Reprinted with permission.

Recommended Journaling

Assertiveness

Complete the assertiveness inventory at the beginning of this section and use it to help determine your assertiveness challenges. Are there certain situations in which you are able to demonstrate assertiveness skills? If so, consider what makes it possible to do so. Think of situations where it is not easy to act assertively and think about why. Are there any irrational beliefs that are responsible for your inability to act in a more assertive manner?

Keep a record of situations that call for assertiveness and times you demonstrate various assertive or nonassertive behaviors. Write about things you handled well and consider things you wish you could have done differently. Reflect upon what was hard or easy. Were you able to keep the content of your message clear and concise? Did you say what you wanted to say? Did you maintain respect for the other person? How were the nonverbal components to your message? Did you maintain eye contact? Were your posture, facial expressions, and tone calm and confident?

Think about what types of outcomes may happen when you act nonassertively, assertively, or aggressively in various situations. Consider how you *feel* when you act in these different manners—both before, during, and afterward. Consider how others respond to these various types of behavior. Think about how you feel when you are the recipient of an assertive versus nonassertive or aggressive message from another.

If being assertive is a challenge for you, make a point to read over the *Personal Bill of Rights* and the *Tenets of an Assertive Philosophy* lists on a daily basis. If any points in these lists feel awkward or untrue for you, write about what stands in the way of believing them. Were there any events or people in your life that prevented you from trusting in these rights? Write your own affirmations regarding your assertiveness goals and say them out loud on a daily basis.

11
Body Image

Questions to Consider

- What is body image?

- How comfortable are you with your body and your appearance?

- Who or what tends to affect your body image?

- What messages did you learn about your body or appearance growing up?

- Do you tend to focus more on aspects of your appearance that you like or on things you see as flaws or imperfections?

- How does body image affect your self-esteem?

Body Image

Body image refers to the mental picture you have and the feelings you hold regarding your physical appearance. Your body image can include both positive and negative feelings and, like self-esteem, can be conceptualized on a continuum from unhealthy to healthy. Feelings about your appearance can fluctuate throughout your life, and body image can be influenced by a variety of things, including society, the media, cultural background, messages from childhood, and various life experiences.

A positive or healthy body image does not mean you look like a beautiful, flawless model with the perfect figure. It means you are content with your physical self the way you are. You have a realistic and accepting perception of your appearance, including your size, shape, and physical traits. You feel proud of your good qualities, but you also accept your flaws without dwelling on them or feeling unworthy because of them.

A negative or unhealthy body image includes a distorted perception of how you look, anxiety over traits you view as imperfect, or feelings of worthlessness due to your appearance. Somebody with a negative body image spends a lot of time feeling concerned about appearance. She may constantly compare herself to others and likely berates herself for not measuring up to images that are actually quite unrealistic; for example, those of models that are altered and airbrushed to achieve perfection.

Preoccupation with physical flaws and struggles with a negative body image cultivate low self-esteem and can also lead to serious problems, such as depression or unhealthy exercise and eating habits. In severe cases, there is a potential for obsession with plastic surgery, development of dangerous eating disorders, or use of self-injurious behaviors.

Body image and self-esteem are often related and intertwined. Again, it is hard to say which comes first, but the two undoubtedly affect and reinforce one another. Someone with healthy self-esteem tends to view her appearance in a healthy, realistic manner, while somebody with low self-esteem will often focus unnecessarily on things she views as wrong with her body, continuing to diminish her self-esteem with self-depreciating remarks about her looks.

Just like with low self-esteem, individuals with a negative body image frequently engage in negative self-talk, both internally and vocally. The distorted and negative messages are regarding body parts and physical appearance. Self-talk includes statements like, "I'm fat," "I'm too skinny," "I would look better if I were taller," "If only I had blond hair," "I hate my curly hair," "My breasts are too (big, small, saggy)," "I look like crap," and "I'm ugly." The messages sometimes extend into further irrational beliefs, with thoughts like, "I'll never get married,"

"Nobody will accept me," "I can't compete with ____," and "Who would ever want to date me?" Each time you allow yourself to engage in negative self-talk or make negative statements about your appearance, you chip away at your self-esteem. The worse you feel about yourself, the more you beat yourself up about your appearance, creating yet another destructive cycle.

Body Image & the Media

Body image has become a popular topic of discussion in various fields over the past several decades, especially as it relates to the media and its influence on how individuals view their own bodies. In American society, we are constantly bombarded with images of gorgeous, size zero, busty women used in advertising to sell anything from beer to becoming a vegetarian. (I recently saw an ad of a sexy, naked, skinny blond woman lying on a pile of red peppers and the caption was, "Spice up your life. Go Vegetarian.") While ads like this serve their purpose of capturing attention and promoting consumerism and causes, the constant barrage of sex symbols and seemingly flawless models makes it especially difficult for real people to accept their own bodies. Many of us see these ads and subconsciously buy into the unrealistic standards portrayed. We wind up with a fear of aging, an obsession with being thin, and a belief that we must look perfect at all times in order to be "good enough." The strict criterion society imposes regarding appearance is further illustrated by the amount of wrinkle cream, make-up, and weight loss ads we see on TV and in magazines.

In her thought-provoking series of *Killing Us Softly* documentaries,[*] Jean Kilbourne talks about our culture's advertising and the fact that the body type most often portrayed as acceptable and desirable is one that fewer than five percent of American women actually have. Kilbourne further discusses how problematic and demoralizing the impracticable standards portrayed in modern advertising can be. She remarks that girls are encouraged to "aspire to become nothing" by "this relatively new size in women's clothing—size 0 and size 00."

In *Killing Us Softly 4,* Kilbourne says, "Our popular culture seems to have the ability to make women anywhere and everywhere feel absolutely terrible about themselves." The *Killing Us Softly* documentaries offer numerous visual examples of the kinds of images we are exposed to and provide an eye-opening look at how being inundated with these images can have a negative impact on the self-esteem and psychological well-being of viewers. Kilbourne mentions Anne E. Becker's 1998 study, which showed that the rate of eating disorders in Fiji increased with the introduction of television to the country, and references the American Psychological Association's 2007 report, which concluded that "girls exposed to sexualized images from a young age are more prone to three of the

---

[*] *Excerpts from Jean Kilbourne. (2010). Killing Us Softly 4: Advertising's Image of Women.* [Documentary Film]. Northampton, MA: Media Education Foundation. Used with permission.

most common mental health problems for girls and women—depression, eating disorders, and low self-esteem."

The messages we receive regarding what is considered important, attractive, and desirable can be taxing for any woman, but they are all the more burdensome for women of color. Kilbourne discusses how the challenge to feel acceptable is even greater for women who are not white, saying, "Women of color are generally considered beautiful only if they approximate the white ideal— if they are light skinned, have straight hair, Caucasian features." She points out how the skin of black pop stars is often lightened in advertisements. Further, women from cultural or religious backgrounds that emphasize values contradictory to the "sex sells" nature of our society may face identity confusion and complications in achieving self-acceptance as they struggle to contend with conflicting messages.

The problem with unrealistic and over-sexualized standards in advertising particularly targets women; however, it affects men as well. More and more, the media is filled with images of men with tanned, hairless, and perfectly chiseled bodies. Some men have engaged in steroid use to increase muscle mass and, in recent years, the number of eating disorders has dramatically increased in the male population. In *The Muscular Ideal: Psychological, Social, and Medical Perspectives,* J. Kevin Thompson and Guy Cafri discuss the media's influence in portraying a muscular ideal for men and describe the extremes individuals sometimes go to in order to achieve a certain look, including drug use, cosmetic procedures, and even major surgery.

The concern regarding images of "perfect" men and women is that they set unrealistic criteria for what is considered ideal in terms of appearance. Individuals may aspire to look like the models they see in the media without stopping to realize that these images are often fake and impractical. Advertisements are airbrushed and photoshopped to achieve unrealistic perfection, and it is not readily obvious that the actors and actresses we admire have hair and makeup artists, and the time and resources available to devote to staying in extraordinary shape. Sometimes, one body in an ad will actually be made up of various parts, pieced together from several different models. This creates the false impression that all-over perfection is easily achievable.

One of my favorite examples of the unrealistic messaging we receive in our society regarding ideal body image is that of the Barbie™ doll. In *Body Wars: Making Peace with Women's Bodies,* Margo Maine, Ph.D., talks about the powerful messages that Barbie conveys regarding what our society views as beautiful and desirable. She describes Barbie's characteristics:

Exceptionally tall, but with a child's size three foot permanently molded in a high-heeled position. Barbie's measurements read 39-18-33. Barbie calls this a "full figure," adding that "at 5'9" my happiest weight is 110 pounds." A minimum expected weight for that height is 145 pounds; 110 pounds poses medical risk. Contoured with no body fat or belly, a human Barbie could not menstruate. Her indented ribcage could only be achieved through plastic surgery and the removal of ribs. In fact, Barbie has lost weight since she was created in 1959.

Barbie's accessories, replete with sexy, formfitting outfits, accessories, and games, reinforce her messages about women's bodies. Slumber Party Barbie (1965) came with a bathroom scale permanently set at 110 pounds, and a book, *How to Lose Weight*, with the directions inside, "Don't Eat."[*]

Other sources have talked about Barbie's measurements being so disproportionate that, if she were a real woman, she would be unable to stand up or house all the necessary organs and intestines due to her unrealistically tiny waistline. While the messages Barbie conveys may be subtle, they certainly have the potential to sink into the subconscious minds of little girls, creating the foundation for striving to become something completely unrealistic and unobtainable.

Improving Body Image

In order to improve body image and ultimately increase self-esteem, it is important to work to decrease preoccupation with appearance and end the urge to achieve perfection. Recognize that images in the media are often unrealistic and not worth comparing yourself to. It is also important to pay attention to negative self-talk as it relates to appearance. Many of the internal messages playing through our heads involve dissatisfaction with physical traits. It is difficult to have healthy self-esteem while hating your body or constantly criticizing the way you look. Pay attention to the times you are critical of your appearance and make an attempt to stop focusing on your flaws or the "if onlys" about your appearance.

While it is okay to have goals regarding being fit and looking your best, problems arise when you berate yourself for not being perfect or when your drive to look a certain way overshadows your ability to recognize positive aspects about yourself. In *Killing Us Softly 4,* Jean Kilbourne says, "Now I want to be very clear that there is nothing wrong with wanting to be attractive and sexy. Just about everybody wants this. What's wrong is that this is emphasized for girls and women at incredibly young ages to the exclusion of other important qualities and aspects. Being hot becomes the most important measure of success. And this extremely superficial and limited definition of sexiness makes most women feel insecure and vulnerable, and much less sexy."

When we are bombarded with media and advertising that suggest we must look a certain way to be accepted, respected, and loved, we lose sight of other important aspects of our lives. The perfectionistic drive to obtain the impossible can overshadow our propensity to feel happy and content with our individuality. When the obsession with looking a certain way sets in, it becomes virtually impossible to maintain a sense of healthy self-esteem. Your thinking becomes consumed by thoughts about not being adequate, good enough, or worthy enough.

While it is completely acceptable to put time and effort into your appearance and to push yourself to exercise and look nice, it is important to consider what the motivations behind these endeavors are. The incentive for taking care of yourself ought to be to stay healthy and feel good, rather than to be perfect or "fix" something you see as flawed in order to obtain a sense of worth. Remember that your worth is inherent and not a reflection of how you look or measure up to the various images in pop culture.

Thought-Stopping & Negative Body Image Self-Talk

Pay attention to the self-talk you engage in regarding your body and appearance. Self-esteem is greatly influenced by the messages you say and think in regards to your looks and personal goals around health and appearance. There is a big difference in the impact of the following two thoughts: "I *should* exercise because I'm a fat, lazy slob" versus "I choose to exercise to feel healthy." Watch out for messages that equate your value and worth to your appearance or physical traits.

Notice times you feel upset, anxious, or unhappy about your appearance and consider the specific thoughts behind the negative feelings. Use the thought-stopping method to catch yourself each time you think or say something negative about your looks. Refrain from using harmful words like *ugly, fat,* and *disgusting.* Try instead to focus on positive aspects, incorporating constructive messages about your appearance into your thinking.

Compliment yourself for the traits you feel good about. Say out loud, "I am an attractive person." Even if you do not believe this to be true, begin to say it to yourself on a regular basis. Repetition creates belief and reality. If it is impossible to say something so positive, use one of the bridge phrases, such as "I'm learning to accept my body" and begin repeating this message on a daily basis. Doing so will help you begin to accept yourself as you are, ultimately allowing you to build self-esteem. Eventually you will begin to feel good about your positive qualities and will stop dwelling so much on your flaws.

More Tips for Improving Body Image

- Recognize how much time and energy (and sometimes money!) you spend worrying about your appearance rather than enjoying the moment. Consider what it would be like to put this time and energy into something more productive, like developing a new skill or spending quality time with family and friends.

- As you are decreasing your focus on body image, keep in mind the importance of finding balance between fixating on looks and losing concern altogether. Remember that it is important to put *some* effort into your appearance. When you fail to put any effort into appearance, you are susceptible to feeling depressed and may become stuck in a rut. When you get out of sweatpants and put on a nice outfit, fix your hair, and put on some makeup, you tend to feel better. This is because you send yourself the message that you are worth taking care of. The key here is finding a healthy balance between taking care of yourself and becoming obsessive about appearance. The reasons for tending to your appearance should be because you are important, not because you feel pressure to look or be "good enough."

- Spend time with others who have a healthy body image rather than those who constantly focus on weight and appearance.

- Ensure diversity in your circle of friends and expose yourself to people of all racial and ethnic groups, ages, sizes, and body types. Doing so helps you to recognize and appreciate differences and individuality, making you more accepting of your own individual body type.

- Avoid making comparisons to other women, both real and in the media. Appreciate that every body is unique.

- Give up fashion and entertainment magazines that force concepts and images of the "perfect woman" on you through articles related to beauty, weight loss, and dieting, and through advertisements with stick-thin, flawlessly beautiful models. If you do continue to read these types of magazines, keep in mind that the models have been completely made up for the shoots and then airbrushed to create perfection. Thighs and waists are made to appear skinnier and flyaway hairs, moles, and blemishes are retouched out. Refrain from comparing yourself to these unrealistic images.

- Oftentimes we judge certain body parts individually. We focus on our thighs as being too fat, our noses as being too big, our breasts as being too small, or our faces as having too many wrinkles. Rather than focusing on "trouble areas," try to view your body as a whole and see it as unique and valuable, rather than as separate parts in need of improvement.

- Make an effort to take good physical care of yourself by eating well and exercising regularly. When you make an effort to take care of yourself, you feel better. Again, you give yourself the message that you are worth it. For many people, exercise is not only a way of taking care of their physical appearance, but it is also a way of caring for their mental well-being. Exercise helps to reduce stress and anxiety and helps to fight depression. When you choose to eat healthfully or to exercise, think about how you are nurturing your body and taking good care of your physical appearance *and* emotional health. View it as a healthy choice, rather than a "should" or "have to." Praise yourself for your efforts.

- As you pay attention to diet and exercise, remember the importance of doing things in moderation. Be sure to avoid extremist behaviors, such as working out obsessively or becoming too rigid by denying yourself the occasional break, treat, or dessert.

- Do not worry about the number on the scale. Remember that muscle weighs more than fat, so if you are working out, your weight may remain relatively unchanged as you lose fat but build and tone muscles. Focus more on how healthy and in-shape you *feel* rather than on achieving a certain weight or size.

- Embrace your "womanhood" by accepting your curves.

- Consider the importance of variety in your workout routines. If you have a mixture of different exercise activities to choose from, you are less likely to get bored and will have options in terms of what fits with your schedule, availability, and mood on any given day.

- As you set exercise goals, remember the importance of keeping goals realistic and obtainable. It is better to set small goals and stay motivated when you reach them than it is to become discouraged by failing to meet goals that are too overly optimistic.

- Two books that are useful for women struggling with body image issues are *Eating in the Light of the Moon* by Anita Johnston and *Body Wars: Making Peace with Women's Bodies* by Margo Maine.

Recommended Journaling

Body Image

In your journal, write about your current state in terms of body image. Do you feel your own body image is healthy or unhealthy? What experiences and which people have shaped your present feelings about your body and appearance? What have you witnessed in others in terms of how they regard their own looks?

How would you assess your overall physical health? Do you have healthy eating habits? Do you exercise regularly? How much time and effort do you put into appearance? What influences the decisions you make regarding caring for your physical health and appearance?

What issues do you have with your body and appearance? Are there certain things you wish you could change? Does preoccupation with these areas tend to affect the overall way you feel about yourself?

Your Idea of the Perfect Woman (or Man):

Consider what your beliefs and ideas are regarding the "perfect" or "ideal" woman. How would you describe her? In your journal, write a description that includes details of the following physical traits:

- Height
- Weight
- Hair color, texture, and length
- Complexion
- Face shape
- Eye color and shape
- Ears
- Nose
- Mouth
- Teeth
- Body shape
- Stomach
- Chest
- Hips
- Buttocks
- Legs

Consider how you compare to your description of the perfect woman. Do you measure up or fall short regarding your view of what is ideal? Think about whether you beat yourself up for feeling inadequate. Do you let distorted beliefs due to your internalized concept of the perfect woman influence your thinking? For example, do you often think, "I *should* be this size," or "If only I had this color hair"? Is your description of the perfect woman realistic and achievable?

How does your concept of the perfect woman affect your self-esteem? What would it take to obtain and maintain these ideals? Where do your ideas of the perfect woman come from? What role do family members, friends, significant others, and the media play in your formation of these ideals? In what areas are you willing to make your criteria for the ideal woman less rigid? What are your priorities in terms of appearance?

Self-Talk and Body Image:

Pay attention to the messages you are thinking and telling yourself regarding your body and appearance. Watch out for distorted thinking, should statements, perfectionist tendencies, and unrealistic goals. Make an effort to say nice things to yourself regarding your physical traits and to practice saying affirmations that help promote a healthy body image.

12

Self-Care

Questions to Consider

- What is self-care?

- How often do you take time out for yourself?

- What type of leisurely, fun, or relaxing activities do you currently engage in?

- In what ways do you pamper or nurture yourself?

- What keeps you from devoting more time to yourself?

- Do you have any irrational thoughts related to giving yourself permission to spend more time engaged in recreational or self-nurturing activities?

- Why is self-care an important part of healthy self-esteem?

Self-Care

Healthy self-esteem involves taking good care of yourself. This means loving yourself and treating yourself well. As we have discussed, the way you talk to yourself is very important in establishing and maintaining healthy self-esteem. Additionally, the subtle, nonverbal messages you send through the ways in which you treat yourself also are important. The degree to which you take care of your overall self can be a direct reflection of how high or low your self-esteem may be. When your self-esteem is low, you tend to neglect your well-being. This lack of attention to self-care may come from beliefs that your needs do not matter or from feeling that you do not deserve time for yourself. Neglecting self-care reinforces low self-esteem because it sends and reinforces messages that you are not important.

Part of building healthy self-esteem involves improving your level of self-care by making healthy choices and taking time out to do things you enjoy. When you regularly engage in activities that keep you healthy and make you feel good, you send the message that you are important. As you begin to add more self-care into your routine, you may need to actively dispute any negative thoughts that try to tell you that you are undeserving or not a priority.

Self-care activities can sometimes feel like a luxury, thus people with low self-esteem may worry that caring for themselves is a sign of selfishness; however, the opposite is true. Self-care is only selfish if you focus on yourself and engage in your own activities 100 percent of the time without concern for the needs of others. Instead, it is important to find a healthy balance between time for yourself and time devoted to helping or caring for others. When you deny yourself time for self-care, you risk depleting your resources and burning out. When this happens, you become cranky, bitter, or just simply too tired to really be there for others. Instead, when we make time to care for ourselves and do the things we enjoy, we refresh our energy and are able to be present for and attentive to those in our lives. We feel better about ourselves and happier, and we are better able to manage stress.

I like the example of oxygen masks on airplanes to demonstrate the importance of self-care: Flight attendants always say, "Put your own oxygen mask on before assisting others." This is because if you run out of oxygen, you will be useless to anyone else. Similarly, if you take a few moments to take care of yourself, you then have the resources available to care for those who need you. The same concept is true with self-care. The idea is that when you make caring for yourself a priority, you end up happier and more energized, and are in a better position to be available to others.

People frequently cite lack of time and difficulty fitting in the "extras" as reasons why they often neglect self-care. When we are busy with family, work, and other obligations, the first things we tend to forgo are those that would be considered self-care activities. We may skip a meal, decline an invitation to spend time with friends, or give up our favorite hobby. By constantly making sacrifices in terms of caring for yourself, you begin to chip away at your self-esteem. You put yourself very low on the priority list and eventually may lose sight of yourself altogether. When you skip or give up self-care, you send the message that you are unimportant and that your needs are insignificant. This subtle message feeds your low self-esteem and is sometimes apparent to others. This is an example of how we convey poor, weak boundaries and teach others how to treat us. When we do not demonstrate self-care as a priority, we send the message that we do not value our own time, happiness, and welfare, which can result in being taken advantage of and neglected by others who follow our lead.

Basic Self-Care Tips

Self-care involves straightforward concepts of maintaining good health, including healthy eating, regular exercise, and enough rest. Eating healthfully means eating foods that are good for you, eating in moderation, listening to your body when it is hungry or full, not skipping meals, and avoiding fad diets that only work temporarily. When it comes to exercise, incorporate a variety of activities into your workout routines and remember to set goals that are realistic. Be sure to get enough rest at night and take time out to relax when you catch yourself feeling overworked. Watch out for the tendency to fall into a "sweatpants slump" where you neglect your appearance because your self-esteem is so low or you are feeling too depressed to care. Paying attention to your physical appearance and putting some effort into getting dressed and made up helps you to feel good about yourself and sends the message that you are important and worth it.

Another important part of self-care involves maintaining a good support network made up of healthy relationships with family and friends. Social outlets, including taking fun classes, joining groups, participating in religious organizations, or having regular get-togethers with others, are also important in terms of preventing isolation and depression. Cut back on time you spend with negative friends or family members who bring you down. Eliminate toxic relationships from your life and use assertiveness to protect self-esteem with those you cannot avoid. Make an effort to spend time with people who bring out your fun side and remember to let yourself laugh. Humor is another simple yet very powerful way to feel good. The saying "Laughter is the best medicine" tends to be true, and the health benefits of humor are well established. When you have healthy self-esteem, you are able to make mistakes without agonizing over them and can sometimes laugh at yourself. Seeing the world and yourself through the lens of humor and having a lighthearted attitude can help you to keep things in perspective and stay positive.

Self-Care Activities

Healthy self-esteem and good self-care involve setting aside time just for you and regularly engaging in activities you enjoy. Self-care activities can range anywhere from simple, free, and easy, like taking a walk or listening to music, to more elaborate, costly, and time-consuming, like getting a massage or going on vacation. They include things that you find enjoyable and do for fun, hobbies and creative projects, or things you do to nurture and pamper yourself—basically anything you enjoy doing that helps you to feel good and relaxed.

Meetup.com is a good website for meeting new people and joining groups focused on all kinds of topics and areas of interest, such as sports teams, hiking, gardening, parenting, and many more. Taking time to develop your creative side or engaging in learning something new is another form of self-care. The Internet is also a great resource for finding classes in your community, such as painting, knitting, dancing, cooking, or creative writing. When utilizing the Internet, joining new groups, or becoming involved in activities with strangers, remember to put your safety first and practice setting healthy boundaries.

Volunteering can also be an excellent self-care activity. While volunteer work involves helping others, the act of volunteering can boost self-esteem by helping you to feel important and good about yourself for making a difference. Be careful of volunteer work that makes you feel taken advantage of or weak in assertiveness. Volunteer because you want to, not because you feel you cannot say no.

It is important to also incorporate some downtime or leisure for yourself into each day. It does not have to be extremely time-consuming. Some days you may be able to devote an hour or more to doing something you enjoy. Other days, five minutes may be all you have to spare, and that is okay. A tiny bit of time is better than none. By consciously making the choice to take a few minutes out for yourself on a regular basis, you send the message that you are important. You end up feeling refreshed and help to prevent exhaustion and burnout.

It is best to have a wide variety of ideas for self-care activities to engage in. This way, you will have plenty to choose from based on your mood and available time on any given day. It doesn't matter what the activities are, it is just important that you begin incorporating something self-care-related into your routine each day.

Examples of Self-Care Activities

- Go for a walk
- Enjoy nature—watch the sunrise, sunset, stars, clouds
- Take a warm bath

- Get a massage
- Get a manicure/pedicure
- Read a book
- Listen to music
- Watch a movie
- Take a trip for a week, weekend, or even just one night
- Garden
- Practice meditation or relaxation techniques (see below)
- Journal
- Take a class or learn something new
- Draw, paint, or do a craft
- Take a nap
- Close your eyes and take some deep breaths
- Enjoy a glass of wine, tea, or coffee
- Play with a pet
- Go to a sports event, concert, or play
- Spend time with a friend

These are examples of some activities that people commonly enjoy and consider self-nurturing activities. Each person's list of self-care activities will be unique. As you make a list of your own self-care activities, consider ones you already engage in and enjoy, as well as those you would like to find time to do. Make an effort to do at least one thing per day from your self-care list, even if it is just for five minutes. Doing so will help you to feel refreshed and will help to build self-esteem. Caring about yourself means remembering to nurture yourself by making time for things you enjoy.

Relaxation Techniques

Relaxation techniques are simple, mindful activities you can do to create a state of relaxation, while decreasing stress, anxiety, and tension. With practice and regular use, relaxation techniques can become excellent self-care activities and can help you to enjoy a better quality of life.

While you cannot always avoid stress, you can learn ways to counteract the negative effects of stress on your mind, body, and spirit. When you become stressed, your body often reacts by releasing chemicals that prepare you for the "fight or flight" response. While this response is useful in emergency situations, regular activation of these chemicals can wear you down. Relaxation techniques can help you to restore balance in your body by creating actual physiological responses, including a reduction in stress hormones, heart rate, and blood pressure, and an increase in oxygen to the brain and blood flow to major muscles. Mentally, relaxation techniques can restore your sense of calmness and help you to feel more relaxed and grounded.

Research shows that regular use of relaxation techniques can also increase energy and focus, heighten problem-solving skills, boost motivation and productivity, combat illness, relieve aches and pains, and result in a better night's sleep. Regularly engaging in relaxation techniques can also help to fight depression and anxiety. Following are examples of some common relaxation techniques:

Deep Breathing

Deep breathing is a simple technique that focuses on taking slow, deep, cleansing breaths. Although extremely simple, this technique can feel very strange and unnatural at first; however, with practice it can become a useful tool that can be used almost anywhere, in any situation. It can provide a quick way to decrease feelings of stress on both the mind and body.

Normally, breathing seems easy. It is something we all do without even thinking about it. If you watch a baby sleep, you will notice how the baby's belly rises and falls with each breath. This is the way we are all meant to breathe— from our diaphragm, with full, deep breaths. Babies instinctively breathe this way; however, as we grow older and face the challenges and stressors of life, our breathing often becomes more shallow.

This is especially true during times of stress or when we are rushed with constant activity and busy schedules. This shallow breathing is counteractive to being able to relax and stay calm and focused. In times of extreme anxiety, shallow breathing can result in panic attacks. When we do not use our lungs' full capacity, blood vessels can become constricted, and there can be an imbalance between oxygen and carbon dioxide levels. This imbalance can result in less oxygen being delivered to the brain, the heart, and the rest of the body. An imbalance in oxygen and carbon dioxide can contribute to feelings of fatigue, depression, and anxiety, and can result in a buildup of toxins that should have been eliminated through exhalation.

Learning to take slow, deep breaths can be extremely helpful in decreasing feelings of stress and anxiety in the moment and in the long-term prevention of adverse physical and psychological consequences. Deep breathing may feel awkward and forced at first; however, practicing this technique can be a useful way to retrain yourself to breathe in a manner that helps to you to best manage the stressors in your life.

As you first begin practicing deep breathing, do it regularly and during times when you are fairly calm. Without practice, if you first try deep breathing when you are already anxious, you may end up hyperventilating and increasing the anxiety. As you get more accustomed to deep breathing and are able to do it in a controlled manner, you can start applying it during times you notice yourself feeling especially anxious, angry, or stressed. When this happens, pay attention to your breathing and notice whether your breaths are very shallow. If so, make a conscious effort to slow your breathing down gradually and inhale and exhale fully.

An example of when deep breathing works well for me is when I am stuck in bad traffic. As soon as I feel myself becoming frustrated, I stop and focus on my breathing, making a point to breathe in and out very slowly and deeply. The effect I feel on my body is instantaneous. I can literally feel my body relax and my attitude shift from frustration to tolerance. Pairing deep breathing with affirmations can also be helpful. A useful technique is to think certain words, phrases, or affirmations on the inhalations and the exhalations to help you concentrate on focused, slow breathing. The mindfulness of the experience can help calm the negative energy or anxiety you are experiencing.

I once had a professor who used music in her therapy practice. She taught clients to sing to a tune the following: "When I breathe in, I breathe in love. (Inhale.) When I breathe out, I breathe out peace. (Exhale.)" Remembering this tune in my head while practicing deep breathing has helped me to pace my inhalations and exhalations during times of stress.

To Practice Deep Breathing:

- Start by getting into a comfortable position, and take a few moments to relax as much as possible.

- Breathe in slowly and deeply through the nose.

- Hold for a few seconds.

- Then release slowly through the nose or mouth.

- Repeat this pattern of breathing several times.

- It is often useful to imagine yourself inhaling "good things" (calm, peace, joy, happiness, relaxation—whatever you need at the moment) and exhaling "bad things" (stress, frustration, anxiety, anger, pain, etc.)

- When you are first practicing, you may wish to place your hand on your belly to feel it rising and falling with each deep breath. In certain yoga poses, one hand is placed on the belly and the other on the chest. Making sure that the hand on your belly rises slightly above the hand on the chest with each breath can help to ensure that the diaphragm is pulling air all the way into the base of the lungs.

If deep breathing is new to you, begin practicing it on a regular basis. Once you are comfortable with pacing your inhalations and exhalations in whatever way best works for you, you can use deep breathing as a tool or coping mechanism to manage stress and anxiety.

Progressive Muscle Relaxation

Progressive muscle relaxation is another relaxation technique that involves a concentrated effort on the tensing and relaxing of different muscle groups in the body. This technique can be done either in a seated or reclined position. For example, it can be useful if done while sitting at your desk when stressed at work. It can also be useful to do while lying in bed at night, especially if you are having trouble falling asleep.

Progressive Muscle Relaxation Steps:

- Start by getting into a comfortable position, either lying down or seated in a chair with your feet flat on the floor.

- Take a few moments to relax as much as possible, breathing in and out deeply.

- Shift your attention to your feet and take a moment to feel how they feel, planted on the ground or lying on the bed.

- Next, tense both of your feet, squeezing your muscles tightly. (You can do both the right and left sides at the same time, or, if you have more time, you can do this activity by focusing on one side at a time.)

- Hold your muscles tensed in this position for a few seconds. (Five to ten seconds is usually a good amount of time, but you can choose the length that works best for you.)

- Next, relax your feet slowly, feeling the tension flowing away as your muscles become relaxed and loose.

- Follow the same sequence of tensing, holding, then relaxing your muscles, moving slowly up through your body (do your feet, calves, thighs, hips/buttocks, abdomen, back, shoulders, hands, arms, neck, and face).

At the end of the muscle relaxation exercise, you should feel more relaxed. Often we store tension in various places in our body without even realizing it; for example, in the jaw. Progressive muscle relaxation can help you to recognize where you are holding tension and allow you the opportunity to release it. The more you practice progressive muscle relaxation, the more familiar you will become with where your body stores tension. With this awareness, you can make a better effort to release tension before it builds up.

Body Scan

Body scanning is a technique similar to progressive muscle relaxation; however, instead of tensing and releasing muscles, you simply focus your attention on various parts of the body, working your way up from the tips of your toes to the top of your head or vice versa. Like progressive muscle relaxation, you start in a comfortable position—lying down seems to be the most relaxing; however, you can do this seated as well. Start with your feet and work your way up the body, individually focusing on each body part, noticing how it feels at that moment.

It may be useful to imagine all the work that body part does or has done that day, then concentrate on letting it relax and be completely still. You may also find it useful to imagine each body part feeling either really heavy or really light as you work your way up the body. For example, you could imagine each body part being covered in sand, making it feel really heavy and weighed down. Or you could imagine each body part being light as a feather, floating slightly above the surface where you are laying/sitting. Try a few different ways and determine which is the most relaxing to you. By the time you have worked your way from the bottom up, you will likely feel calmer and more relaxed.

Meditation

Meditation is one very simple, easy, readily available self-care activity that can be highly beneficial and relaxing. Some people tend to be turned off by the word *meditation* because they envision devout monks sitting silently in uncomfortable positions for hours at a time. However, meditation is really just about allowing your brain to rest for a few moments.

Merriam-Webster's Collegiate® Dictionary provides the following definitions for the word *meditate:* "to spend time in quiet thought for religious purposes or relaxation; to engage in contemplation or reflection; to engage in mental exercise (as concentration on one's breathing or repetition of a mantra) for the purpose of reaching a heightened level of spiritual awareness; to focus one's thought on; reflect on or ponder over…"* While meditation can be linked to religious traditions and can include some intense practices, meditation is really just about training your mind to focus and be calm, which can be an important component to learning to control negative self-talk. Meditation techniques are great because there are lots of variations to test out and they can be done almost anywhere, for any length of time you choose.

In *Learn to Meditate: A Practical Guide to Self-Discovery and Fulfillment*, David Fontana, Ph.D., defines meditation as "the experience of the limitless nature of the mind when it ceases to be dominated by its usual mental chatter." He explains that the mind "represents our true nature, a nature that is naturally calm and serene, unclouded by the various anxieties and wishes, hopes and fears that usually occupy our attention." Meditation can be an excellent way to quiet your mind and practice shutting out all of the negative self-talk for a few moments a day. The more you practice meditation, the easier it will become to gain control over your mind and thoughts.

There are many different meditation "techniques," and some that may be relaxing to one person may be anxiety-provoking for another. Some involve focusing on an object, while others involve repeating a certain word, mantra, or affirmation. There are even different forms of movement and walking meditations. Some meditation methods utilize various visual tools to help you release unwanted or stressful thoughts. One that I like involves imagining your intrusive thoughts (or negative self-talk messages) floating out of your mind and into balloons or bubbles that take them far away out into space.

Another that I frequently use when I get fixated on a specific distracting and unhelpful thought is to imagine myself placing that thought into a box that I then place in the back of a closet. I literally imagine myself putting the thought in the box, placing it on the shelf in the closet, then closing the closet door and walking away. I know that thought is still there and I can deal with it later, when I have more time and energy; but, for the moment, I can put the thought to rest and allow the box to hold it for me so my mind can focus on others things. This visualization can be especially useful at night when you are trying to fall asleep but find your mind is racing with thoughts that are keeping you awake, or when you catch yourself ruminating over a mistake or imperfection. Just imagine yourself putting those thoughts in the box, where you can pick them up again later.

It may take some practice and trial and error to find the techniques that work best for you. The goal is to find some form of meditation that serves as a relaxing tool for you. When you find something that works, add it to your self-care-activities list and practice it regularly.

---

* By permission from *Merriam-Webster's Collegiate® Dictionary, 11th Edition* © 2014 by Merriam-Webster, Inc. (www.Merriam-Webster.com)

There are many resources available that teach and facilitate meditation. The Chopra Center (www.chopra.com) frequently provides free "21-Day Meditation Experiences" that allow you to listen to different guided meditations each day on various topics. There are also numerous CDs, downloadable tracks on iTunes, cell phone apps, and podcasts available that help you practice meditation. Sleep Machine is a smartphone app that I like. It allows you to choose various soothing melodies and set them to a timer. Listening to one of the sounds for five minutes a day as you close your eyes and relax can be a great self-care activity. For more, see www.meganmaccutcheon.com/relaxation.

Mindfulness

Mindfulness is an important part of meditation and is often referred to as an ideal in terms of an overall way of being. Mindfulness involves being aware of our thoughts, emotions, and physical sensations in the present moment. Being mindful of feelings, both emotional and physical, and of thoughts is a necessary component to monitoring self-talk. There are lots of mindfulness practices out there to help you to develop and become more familiar with this skill. For example, try being more mindful as you eat. Pay attention to various sensations and your senses as you take a bite. How does the food smell? How does it taste? What is the texture of various foods like in your mouth? Chew slowly and really become aware of what it is like to be eating the meal.

Daily Om: Inspirational Thoughts for a Happy, Healthy, and Fulfilling Day, by Madisyn Taylor, is one example of a book that provides short, mindful readings that may help you to begin practicing mindfulness in everyday situations. Try reading one of these thoughts each day or sign up at www.dailyom.com to receive daily inspirational thoughts in your email. There are many books, websites, and other resources like this out there. See the References & Recommended Reading section at the end of this book or www.meganmaccutcheon.com/mindfulness for more resources. The more you practice mindfulness, the easier it will become to recognize and understand various physical sensations and emotions that relate to different forms of self-talk.

Imagery

Imagery (also called visualization) is a meditative way to relax by imagining a scene that helps you to feel calm and at peace. Choose a location, scene, or setting which you find peaceful. Examples include a beach, the woods, a grassy meadow with wildflowers, a scenic spot on a mountain, a favorite childhood spot, wrapped in a blanket in front of a cozy fireplace, etc. Start by getting into a comfortable position, either seated or lying down. Close your eyes and try to relax your body as much as possible. Imagine yourself in the setting of your choice, concentrating on how your body and your various senses experience the scene.

You can do imagery on your own using your imagination or by using an audio recording of a guided meditation, often called "guided imagery." There are many different types of guided visualizations available. Some involve imagining a special place, some utilize visualizing various colors, and some ask you to imagine a wise guide giving you answers to your questions. The main goal of guided imagery is relaxation, but there can be many other beneficial uses. There have even been reports of how visualization has helped individuals heal from certain ailments or fight off various diseases.

Below is an example of a guided imagery script using a beach setting. Read this script to yourself, then close your eyes and try to play through a similar sequence of deep breathing, body scan, and visualization on your own. Alternatively, you may wish to practice with a friend by reading the script to each other. You can also create your own guided visualization by reading the script out loud into an audio recorder, then playing it back to yourself. Remember to speak slowly and pause between sentences so there will be plenty of time for you to relax as you listen to the recording. The beach is typically a relaxing setting for most people; however, if your association with the beach is traumatic or unsettling, you can replace the beach references with a different setting.

———•———

Beach Guided Imagery

Close your eyes and get comfortable, releasing any tension from your body.... Relax your muscles as much as possible.... Breathe in deeply, in through your nose.... And out.... Breathe slowly in.... And out.... Repeat these deep breaths a few more times.

Feel yourself releasing tension from your body with each exhale, replacing it with relaxation through each breath.... Let your feet relax.... And your legs.... Allow your legs to be limp.... And let your torso relax.... Let your stomach relax, feeling your belly rise and fall as you continue to breathe in deeply.... Now let your shoulders relax.... And allow your back to relax as much as possible.... Let your arms and hands relax.... Shake your arms a bit and let them go limp.... Let your neck and head relax.... Let your face and jaw relax, making sure you are not storing any tension in those muscles.... Let your entire body rest heavily on the surface where you sit or lie.

Continue to breathe deeply in through your nose, drawing air fully into your lungs.... Exhale slowly, releasing any lingering tension out with your breath…. Continue to breathe in and out deeply…. Become more and more relaxed with each breath….

You may have various thoughts come into your mind…. Let these thoughts pass through your mind…. You can always return to them later…. Let any distracting sounds fade away, only deepening your level of relaxation.

Now imagine you are lying on a gorgeous beach…. The beach is wide and long…. It is empty, calm, and peaceful…. It is a beautiful, sunny day with a beautiful, clear blue sky…. The air is warm and there is a refreshing breeze…. Feel the breeze against your skin…. Imagine you are lying on a soft blanket in the warm sand…. Feel the weight of your body melting into the sand…. You feel the smooth sand graze your fingertips…. The water is crystal clear…. You can smell the fresh ocean spray…. And you can hear the sound of the waves calmly rolling over the sand…. Feel the warmth of the sun on your face….

As you lay peacefully on the beach, you soak up the warm sun and the fresh air, breathing in tranquility and relaxation…. Let all your worries float away…. Let the waves carry your stress, tension, anxieties, and fears far out into the ocean….

Continue to imagine yourself lying peacefully on the beach, breathing in the good things that you need in your life—peace, harmony, love, joy, happiness, hope…. Breathe out the things that weigh you down—tension, stress, anxiety, worry, depression, sadness, fear…. Continue to breathe in and out slowly, feeling increasingly more peaceful.

When you are ready, open your eyes and return to the present moment, leaving behind the beach but keeping with you the feelings of peace and relaxation.

———•———

Tapping

Tapping, also called the Emotional Freedom Technique, is a psychological acupressure technique frequently used to diminish anxiety and improve emotional health. The idea is that there are various pressure points or meridians in our bodies that store emotion and energy. By tapping on these points, we can release anxiety and calm our nervous system.

Nine major tapping points are:

- On the edge of the hand, below the pinkie finger.
- The top of the head.
- The inside points of the eyebrow.
- The outer sides of the eyes (temples).
- Under the eyes.
- Under the nose.
- The chin.
- The collarbone.
- Under the arms.

To use this tool, simply tap lightly with the pads of your fingers on the points. Various resources advocate different or very specific patterns and methods for tapping. Overall, I have found that the most important thing is determining which pressure points work best for you and remembering to utilize tapping when you feel anxiety coming on. Pairing tapping with deep breaths and positive self-talk or affirmative statements can be especially useful.

When I first learned about tapping, I thought it sounded a little crazy but I decided to try it out before giving the toast at my sister's wedding. As it was getting closer to toast time, I began to feel my anxiety increasing, so I asked the wedding coordinator to give me a heads-up about 15 minutes before it was time for my toast. When she did, I went into a bathroom stall and spent a few minutes tapping on my collarbone while saying, "I am calm. I speak clearly. I do fine." After a few minutes of tapping and deep breathing, I felt an immediate shift in my anxiety level and I became a believer in tapping. (Note that my affirmative statements were in the present tense and positive, rather than negative, such as "I am not nervous," or future-oriented, such as "I am going to do great." Stating affirmations in the present tense gives them more power and helps you to feel as if the end goal is already achieved.)

I have also found that tapping on the outside of the hand is especially useful, as it can be done in your lap just about anywhere in a pretty discrete manner. Tapping can be a really great tool for children, as well. I have taught it to several children I have worked with and some have reported finding it helpful to do in school, especially right before or during tests.

Although tapping can seem a little strange or too simplistic at first, with practice, it can become an excellent tool for managing stress and inducing a state of relaxation. It can even help to decrease anxiety and stop panic attacks. When you concentrate on tapping, your focus is on being mindful and taking care of yourself, which can help to improve self-esteem and your overall sense of well-being.

Tips for Enhancing Relaxation

One way to enhance and deepen your experience while practicing relaxation techniques is to engage your senses. Breathing in the smell of scented oils or candles can be very relaxing. Lavender, for example, is an especially calming fragrance. Repeated use of a certain smell can help train your brain to relax in the presence of that scent.

Soft, calm music is also very helpful in allowing your mind and body to relax. Using sound machines or playing instrumental "spa music" is another great way to augment relaxation experiences. Pairing specific sounds with certain visualizations can help you feel more connected to the imagery. For example, many sound machines feature an "ocean waves" sound, which can enhance the experience of the beach guided imagery script earlier in this chapter.

Comfortable pillows and blankets can help you to feel cozy and pampered. Using an eye pillow over your eyes as you relax or meditate can help to deepen your concentration and make you feel more peaceful. I especially like ones that are scented with lavender or rose petals, as they can also engage your sense of smell to heighten relaxation.

Many people find that creating a tranquil, serene place or "sanctuary" in their home can help encourage time for meditation or relaxation. It does not have to be elaborate. It can be as simple as gathering a few candles, a soft blanket, a scented eye pillow, and an iPod with some soothing sounds, and devoting a corner, drawer, or box to housing your "relaxation tools."

It may be useful to incorporate meditation or relaxation techniques into your daily routine. Practicing them often will help you to determine what works and will allow you to tailor various exercises in ways that make them work best for you. Once you are familiar with these techniques, you may find them helpful to employ during stressful times throughout your day. For example, deep breathing can be helpful if you become stressed out or frustrated at work, during a conflict with a family member, or while waiting in a long line. Body scans or guided imagery may help people to let go of tension or fall asleep more quickly at night.

Remember that meditation and relaxation techniques take practice. At first, they can feel a little hokey or even extremely awkward and unnatural. It is normal to feel a little skeptical in the beginning; however, with practice, relaxation techniques will feel more natural and can prove to be extremely helpful in managing everyday stress and anxiety. Set your expectations low at first and do not put too much pressure on yourself to immediately feel a deep level of peace or to silence your mind. It may take a lot of practice to truly experience the benefits and calming effects of these exercises. The great news about meditation and relaxation techniques is that they are relatively easy to practice on your own—anytime, anywhere. I personally recommend using the last few minutes of the day, before you fall asleep at night, to try some of these techniques. Doing so will give you practice and might also help you to fall asleep faster and sleep better.

Creative Outlets

Many people find various creative or artistic outlets to be extremely fun, fulfilling, and relaxing. There are all kinds of creative hobbies and activities that can be considered avenues for self-care—arts and crafts, painting, drawing, writing, gardening, drama, riddles, crossword puzzles. If you enjoy artistic or creative activities, incorporate them into your self-care repertoire. Some especially therapeutic ideas follow:

Journaling

Journaling can be very cathartic and an excellent way to process your thoughts and emotions. Getting thoughts out of your head and onto paper really helps people to work through various issues. Journaling can be done in any way you find helpful. A simple notebook or even scrap paper is all you really need; however, some people enjoy writing in a journal that has a pretty cover or a lock and key. Other people dislike their handwriting or are quicker at typing and prefer to journal on the computer in a word processing document. Many people even use a notes app on their smartphones and are able to journal anywhere, anytime. If you are worried about privacy, you can find various options for password-protected journal or blogging sites through a Google search. You can even throw away, shred, or burn your writing as soon as you have finished it. The main purpose of journaling is to have an outlet for processing and purging various thoughts and feelings.

In *Loving Him Without Losing You: How to Stop Disappearing and Start Being Yourself*, Beverly Engel talks about the usefulness of journaling. She says, "Your journal can act as a silent companion that listens without judgment and reflects back to you aspects of yourself you are unaware of." I have always found that there is something about putting your thoughts and feelings into writing that allows them to flow more freely, often revealing things you did not even realize were in your subconscious.

Journaling can be in any form, including full-sentence paragraphs, jotted-down ideas, or stream-of-consciousness thoughts. You can also incorporate or utilize artistic methods, such as sketching, drawing, or making collages. Some people enjoy writing poetry or song lyrics.

When journaling, you can write about anything you want. People often like to journal on a daily basis by keeping a log of what they did during the day. Jotting down positive aspects of yourself or small accomplishments each day can help with building self-esteem. Gratitude journals are popular and a nice way to focus on the positive aspects or blessings in your life. Some people choose to use journaling only when they have a specific question or problem they need help processing. There is no correct way to journal. Try different things and do whatever you find the most useful.

Regardless of what format or ways you choose to journal, be sure to watch out for perfectionist tendencies or rigid rules that keep the experience from being helpful. Do not worry about things like spelling, grammar, and punctuation, and avoid being too strict about how and when you "should" journal. Remember that journaling is meant to be a self-care tool to give you perspective and a sense of peace. Following are some recommended journaling activities and exercises you may find helpful.

Sentence Completion

In *The Six Pillars of Self-Esteem,* Nathaniel Branden talks about sentence completion as an exercise to help you process and work through various problems in order to achieve better self-understanding. Begin with a sentence stem regarding the issues you are dealing with. For example, "Assertiveness is difficult for me because…" or "If I am more accepting of myself…" or "The reasons I feel stuck are…" Then, as quickly as possible without stopping to reflect, write out as many endings to the sentence as you can over the next few minutes. Do not worry if what you write is true, profound, or makes sense. Just write something, anything that comes to mind, and let your words flow onto the paper. You will likely be surprised by some of the things that come up. This exercise can be useful in terms of bypassing blocks, avoidances, and denial to access what is truly in your subconscious. It can help you to uncover your hidden fears, thoughts, and struggles, allowing you to begin reflecting on the things you need to work through in order to move forward.

Letter Writing

Letter writing is also an especially helpful form of journaling that can aid you in processing feelings or expressing certain desires that are otherwise difficult to convey within a relationship. When writing a letter, the point is to get your bottled-up emotions out and onto paper, or to work through and put into words things you wish you could express. The experience is just for you. Sometimes you may choose to actually deliver the letter (or some edited version of it). Other times, shredding or burning the letter will be the most helpful. Letter writing is a tool that can help you process and release emotions in a healthy way, because in a journal letter, you can say whatever you want in whatever way you need to without concern for the other person's reaction.

Letter writing and other similar exercises are particularly beneficial when an individual needs help processing painful events or working through difficult emotions and situations. Writing letters can be especially useful in working through situations where there are poor boundaries and dysfunctional behaviors, like abuse or neglect. In these circumstances, it is generally unfeasible to express feelings and be heard in a constructive way because healthy communication is difficult or impossible. Thus, letter writing or journaling exercises can provide an outlet for working through emotions. To use the letter writing method, just start with "Dear X" and let whatever you want to say flow. People are often surprised by what comes up when they take the time to put their thoughts onto paper or into a letter.

To take this exercise a step further, you may also try writing a response letter from the person to you. Write whatever you wish they would say to validate your feelings and acknowledge what you have said in your letter. This letter may be completely off base from how the person would actually respond, but that is okay. This is an exercise just for you to give yourself the validation you need and to work through what it is you deeply desire. Sometimes these response letters can be a powerful way to demonstrate the other person's faults, allowing you to release yourself from blame. Letter writing can also be done to and from inanimate objects. For example, some people have found great peace in writing letters to their tumors or cancer and responding from the perspective of the disease back to themselves. Though it may sound strange, try it and you may be surprised what you put on paper.

List Making

Sometimes you may prefer to write lists instead of letters. In *Making Peace with Your Parents: The Key to Enriching Your Life and All Your Relationships,* Harold Bloomfield suggests that people who have challenging relationships with their parents or past can process feelings of resentment by making a list of each painful memory, hurtful incident, or negative feeling by describing them each as specifically as possible.[*] For example, "I resent feeling like you never wanted me to be born," "I resent that you wouldn't stop drinking even though you knew what it was doing to the rest of us," or "I resent that you got divorced." The purpose of the list is for you to let out and release the negative feelings that have been stored inside you for a long time by putting those emotions into words. Exercises like this can help in any relationship and with any

---

[*] See Harold Bloomfield's *Making Peace with Your Parents: The Key to Enriching Your Life and All Your Relationships.* Copyright © 1983 by Bloomfield Productions, Inc. Balantine Books, a division of Random House, Inc., New York.

type of conflict. Lists such as these are just for you to process feelings, not something you need to share unless you choose to do so.

Vision Boards

Vision boarding is an artistic tool you can use to help hone in on some of the wishes, hopes, and dreams you have for yourself and for your life. It is based on the same Law of Attraction that is the driving force behind affirmations. Making a vision board serves as a creative outlet and results in a piece that is essentially like one big visual affirmation. As you are working to build self-esteem and improve self-care, you may find it very helpful, therapeutic, and uplifting to create a vision board that incorporates some of the things you envision or hope to see in your future.

To create a vision board, start by thumbing through a stack of magazines and cutting out any pictures, words, phrases, and quotes that appeal to you or that speak to things you want for yourself. For example, a "Self-Esteem and Self-Care Vision Board" may have words and phrases like *balance, wellness, happiness, make peace with imperfections,* and *I'm a natural beauty.* It might include pictures of places you want to go and things you enjoy doing to care for yourself—pictures of the beach, something that represents serenity, a bubble bath, a yoga pose, or a happy smile. Cut out as many things as you can until you have a nice pile of clippings and are ready to start the board.

You will then need to choose a surface or background. It can be anything you want—a piece of paper, a poster board, a foam core board, a corkboard, a picture frame. Start going through your pile of pictures and laying out what you want to include on your board. You might use everything you cut out and you might not. If there are things you really want to include but could not find in the magazines, you can draw them or find pictures on the computer to print out. When you are happy with the pictures you want to include, glue, tape, or pin them down.

The process of creating a vision board can be really fun and the end result can be an inspirational visual representation of what you are working toward. People have used vision boards to convey all types of dreams and aspirations. Some people put pictures of dream homes and cars, while others may put words like *promotion* or *cancer-free.*

I once created a "Baby Vision Board" during my journey to conceive my first child. It did not seem to be happening and my doctors said the next step was infertility treatment. One night, while feeling particularly discouraged, I decided to stop focusing on the disappointment and on the words *infertility treatments.* Instead, I sat down with a stack of magazines and began cutting out everything baby-related that I could find. Words like *baby, bump, pregnant, baby joy, baby shower, kids, birth, parenting,* and *a baby on the way.* I found pictures of adorable babies, strollers, car seats, cribs, bibs, and baby toys and glued everything onto a piece of foam core board. I became pregnant the following month without any drugs or procedures. While the vision board may not have been the magic solution, the act of envisioning my goals helped me to shift my focus and state of mind from sadness to enthusiasm. The similar shift in attitude is necessary when working to build self-esteem.

Vision boards may not always have immediate results, but they can be incredibly powerful. They tap into your creativity and also help you to verbalize and convey in a visual way what it is you want in your life. Creating a vision board related to your goals for increased self-esteem and an improved quality of life can be a great self-care activity that allows you to focus on yourself, your needs, wants, and desires. For some people who are stuck in a rut, it may be one of the main things that helps motivate them in moving forward on the journey to improving self-esteem.

Self-Care: Make Your Own List

The ideas presented in this chapter include things that have worked well for me or for my clients. They are just a few ideas out of thousands. Make your own list that includes things you already consider self-care activities as well as new things you would like to try, then make an effort to do at least one thing a day. It does not matter what you do, it is just important that you do something healthy and rewarding every day to treat yourself with the respect and attention you deserve.

Recommended Journaling

Self-Care

Create your own list of self-care activities. Consider things you currently do that you find relaxing, fun, or rewarding. Also add activities you would like to do or try. Make sure your list has a wide variety of items to choose from, including simple, quick things as well as longer, more involved endeavors. Make a point to do one activity from your list every day, even if you only have five minutes. Plan ahead to make time for the more involved activities you hope to try.

If you are unable to find time for self-care most days of the week, write about what stands in your way. Consider how you can use assertiveness and better boundaries to ask for help or rearrange your roles and responsibilities in order to make self-care a priority. Think about which irrational beliefs or negative self-talk messages prevent you from taking better care of yourself. Come up with affirmative statements that you can use to help you feel important and deserving of time to yourself.

13

Breaking the Cycle & Fostering Healthy Self-Esteem in Children

Questions to Consider

- If you have children or work with children in some capacity, what type of messages do you hope to convey to them regarding self-esteem?

- How can parents, teachers, and role models encourage positive self-esteem in children?

Breaking the Cycle & Fostering Healthy Self-Esteem in Children

Every time I teach a Building Self-Esteem workshop, somebody always comments, "I wish I had learned this stuff in grade school!" The concepts and tools for building self-esteem are simple, yet they are often things we do not directly learn until we find ourselves in a bad place, facing depression, anxiety, and other negative experiences. Some people never recognize a problem or never seek help and, thus, never learn these tools. They model the negative self-talk and unhealthy behaviors that contribute to low self-esteem and wind up passing these things down from generation to generation.

Others seem to learn the tools for building self-esteem only after going through a significant struggle. Learning these tools later in life may mean it will be more difficult to put them into practice and to break long-standing habits, but the important thing is to recognize that it is possible to challenge and change how you think and behave in order to improve your self-esteem. You now know several of the tools necessary to help raise your self-esteem and improve your overall quality of life. While it is up to you to actively practice these techniques, the awareness of self-talk and importance of assertiveness and self-care is something you likely will not forget. This awareness alone can be a step toward change.

As you put these new tools and skills into practice, you can work on teaching them to your children. By modeling healthy self-esteem and encouraging healthy self-talk, we can provide future generations with the skills and attitudes that will foster their own positive sense of identity. Positive self-esteem in children is a protective measure that helps to prevent them from falling victim to things like depression, anxiety, peer pressure, drug and alcohol abuse, and self-injurious behaviors.

Children are constantly observing and internalizing what goes on around them. You can model positive self-talk and healthy self-esteem through the ways in which you talk about yourself, comment on your mistakes and shortcomings, and demonstrate making yourself a priority. If you have not modeled positive self-esteem and good self-care in the past, start now. You might even use your efforts as talking points with your children and consider starting a conversation about self-esteem: "I'm reading a book (or taking a workshop) on building self-esteem and am really working to treat myself better." Explain self-talk to family members and ask them to help point out times you slip into negative thinking or make disparaging comments about yourself. In having these conversations with family members and friends, you normalize the struggles we all face in recognizing our worth and you demonstrate the importance of valuing yourself.

Acknowledge and validate your children's feelings, both positive and negative, and teach them that it is okay to express a range of emotions. Communicate to them that experiencing feelings is natural and not a choice, but what you do with emotions and how you articulate them is. Remember to praise children for things like effort, determination, perseverance, and making an attempt, not just for perfect grades, winning, and success. Be mindful of the things you say to your children and make sure to give them messages that let them know they are loved, important, and valued. You cannot tell your children enough that you are proud of them and love them unconditionally. The language you use and the messages you send are so important in terms of forming the foundation for the belief system, values, and sense of personal worth that children internalize.

In *Self-Compassion,* Kristin Neff explains, "Many parents don't provide comfort and support, but rather try to control their children through constant criticism." She says, "Research shows that individuals who grow up with highly critical parents in childhood are much more likely to be critical toward themselves as adults. People deeply internalize their parents' criticisms, meaning that the disparaging running commentary they hear inside their own head is often a reflection of parental voices—something passed down and replicated throughout generations." Be cognizant of the language and messages you convey to children, as your words begin to shape their own basis for self-talk and rational versus irrational thinking.

Ensure that your compliments are not actually backhanded criticisms; for example, "Good report card, but you need to pull up that history grade," or "Good game, but you should have taken that shot." Remember that it takes many positive comments to balance out the effects of one negative remark, so give your children constructive praise as often as possible. Be very careful of criticism that is shaming, condescending, or demeaning. In *The Gifts of Imperfection,* Brené Brown says, "Using shame to parent teaches children that they are not inherently worthy of love."

It is natural and human that you will sometimes make mistakes as a parent or teacher, and there will inevitably be times when you lose your cool and say the wrong thing; however, you can use these moments as opportunities to apologize to your children, showing them that it is okay to make mistakes and show imperfections. The more you are able to admit to your own faults and weaknesses, the easier it will be for children to accept that we all make mistakes and have flaws.

Affirm and acknowledge good behaviors and things you appreciate. When children do not get the positive reinforcement they need to build healthy self-esteem, they may begin acting out. Negative reinforcement sometimes feels better than being ignored or unnoticed; however, in the long run, negative reinforcement without an offset of plenty of positive regard creates feelings of shame and poor self-esteem. Be mindful of the language and tone you use to reprimand and set limits with children.

As you practice setting boundaries, remember that children actually need and want structure in their lives. Setting and communicating clear boundaries with children helps them learn responsibility and gives them a sense of stability. One formula that is useful for setting boundaries and following through with consequences is the "If—Then—Since" formula. For example, *"If* you don't pick up the book you threw on the floor, *then* you will go in time-out"…(Wait a few seconds)…"Okay, *since* you did not pick up the book, now you will go to time-out." Then follow through with the consequences you set. This demonstrates a clear boundary that you expect your child to listen to your request and that there will be consequences if they do not. Assertive parenting and strict boundaries can be offset with plenty of love and freedom in other areas.

Remember that if you have not been in the practice of setting clear boundaries, you will likely be met with initial resistance as you start to become firmer in setting and reinforcing limits. But stick with it, and eventually the result will be a smoother, happier dynamic for the whole family. Children do well when they clearly understand the rules and know what to expect.

In regards to body image, talk to children about their bodies and normalize the changes they go through as they grow. Teach them that bodies come in many different shapes, sizes, colors, and varieties. Have conversations about the advertisements and media you observe and explain to them that many of the models and actors they see are not realistic portrayals because models have been made up and altered. Explain to children that worth is not determined by looks or by the opinions and remarks of others.

∽

There is no manual for parenting, yet how we parent and interact with children has a profound impact on their self-esteem and overall development. Even if we are not motivated to make changes to build our own self-esteem and improve our own quality of life, we have a responsibility to model healthy behaviors and interactions for future generations. The following two poems serve as helpful reminders that the words we speak and the behaviors we model create the foundation of self-esteem in the children we interact with. For books related to self-esteem, positive identity, affirmations, and assertiveness geared toward children, see www.meganmaccutcheon.com/kidsbooks.

———◆———

Children Love to Learn When They Learn with Love!*

by Diana Loomans

"I got an A," the young boy said. "All right, hooray for me!"
His teacher frowned and merely said, "You should have gotten three."

"I cleaned the garage," the teen girl said, "and put your tools away."
Her father scowled, and then he said, "That wasn't the right way."

"I've checked off everything on the list," the boy said with a smile.
His mother stated sullenly, "But it took you such a long while."

The children who lived nearby were learning so much more.
They were taught with lots of love, which helped each one to soar.

"I got an A," the young boy said. "All right, hooray for me!"
His teacher beamed and happily said, "You're proud of that, I see!"

"I cleaned the garage," the teen girl said, "and put your tools away."
Her father grinned, and then he said, "You've helped a lot today."

"I've checked off everything on the list," the boy said with a smile.
"Indeed, you have," his mother said, admiring him all the while.

Children need acknowledgment for what they're asked to do.
To learn to love and love to learn, so much depends on you.

———◆———

————◆————

Children Learn What They Live[*]

by Dorothy Law Nolte, Ph.D.

If children live with criticism, they learn to condemn.
If children live with hostility, they learn to fight.
If children live with fear, they learn to be apprehensive.
If children live with pity, they learn to feel sorry for themselves.
If children live with ridicule, they learn to feel shy.
If children live with jealousy, they learn to feel envy.
If children live with shame, they learn to feel guilty
If children live with encouragement, they learn confidence.
If children live with tolerance, they learn patience.
If children live with praise, they learn appreciation.
If children live with acceptance, they learn to love.
If children live with approval, they learn to like themselves.
If children live with recognition, they learn it is good to have a goal.
If children live with sharing, they learn generosity.
If children live with honesty, they learn truthfulness.
If children live with fairness, they learn justice.
If children live with kindness and consideration, they learn respect.
If children live with security, they learn to have faith
in themselves and in those about them.
If children live with friendliness, they learn the world
is a nice place in which to live.

————◆————

Recommended Journaling

**Breaking the Cycle &
Fostering Healthy Self-Esteem in Children**

If you are a parent or someone who works with a younger generation in any capacity, recognize that children are always watching, observing, and learning from our examples. Pay attention to the behaviors, attitudes, and messages you are conveying and consider how the self-esteem of children may be impacted by the ways we treat and speak to them. Make an effort to ensure criticism is constructive and that redirection and punishments are delivered in a manner that is not shaming, belittling, or condescending. Also ensure that you are giving children plenty of positive encouragement and acknowledging them for their efforts, perseverance, and willingness to try new things. Know that children observe and internalize the behaviors and messages we model and be aware of how your own level of self-esteem and your own self-talk messages may impact others.

In your journal, write about how you can help foster healthy self-esteem in children and others. Are there certain things you want to do differently than your parents and role models did? Make a list of positive things you like or admire about a child in your life and make an effort to ensure they are aware of how you feel.

14

Wrapping Up & Ongoing Efforts

Questions to Consider

- What gains have you made in your efforts to build self-esteem?

- What challenges have you found in improving self-esteem and in implementing the recommended tools described?

- How likely are you to continue practicing these tools? What could you do to keep motivated?

- What goals do you have regarding continued efforts to build self-esteem?

Wrapping Up & Ongoing Efforts

Building self-esteem is an ongoing process that takes time and effort. After reading this book, you will have a greater awareness of how your thoughts and behaviors impact your self-esteem. With that awareness comes constant movement forward. Now that you know what self-talk is and understand its pervasive effects, you will find yourself hearing that voice and internal chatter more readily. With a conscious effort to monitor and change negative self-talk and practice the recommended self-esteem-building tools, you can greatly improve the way you feel about and treat yourself.

Improving self-esteem really does involve breaking deep-seated habits; ones that are often so subtle and subconscious that you do not really notice you are doing them until you are forced by depression, anxiety, relationship difficulties, or other chaotic aspects of your life to really consider a need to change. Creating change can be extremely challenging and scary. It involves stepping outside your comfort zone and can sometimes feel like you are swimming upstream. Rather than beat yourself up for encountering obstacles and difficulties in making progress, compliment yourself for being willing to consider a need for change. Remember that change is a process. With commitment and determination, you can create worthwhile results.

The chapters in this workbook have offered various techniques and suggestions for establishing a framework to improve and maintain self-esteem. Using these tools is a lifelong endeavor. Oftentimes, we learn new things and they stick for a few weeks as we stay motivated, but soon we fall back into old patterns and habits, and the techniques that could ultimately help us begin to fade away. This is especially true when life gets busy or we are faced with stressful situations that knock us off track. But it is during these times in particular that things like self-care, healthy self-talk, and maintaining clear boundaries are so very important.

Remember that repetition rewires the brain. By taking every opportunity to practice these techniques all day, every day, you will begin to create a foundation of healthy self-esteem and will become increasingly better at maintaining a new pattern of thinking that will ultimately help you to feel better about yourself. Many of these tools seem fairly simplistic and straightforward; however, they can be hard at first because they are new or in opposition to what you are used to doing. What I like about these tools, especially changing self-talk, is that most really can be done anywhere, anytime. All day long you have opportunities to look at how you are thinking and to contemplate the most effective ways to formulate both your internal and external messages.

When you are able to overcome the habit of negative self-talk and instead utilize rational, healthy self-talk and assertiveness as your norm, you essentially create a shield or a protective barrier that prevents the negativity, criticisms, and rejection of others from harming your foundation of self-esteem. Remember that it takes several positive messages to outweigh a negative one, so take every opportunity you can to give yourself positive, affirmative messages in addition to blocking or changing the negative ones.

No matter how great you are with practicing healthy self-talk and developing better boundaries and assertiveness, there will inevitably be times when you slip up. We are all faced with challenging events and circumstances that force us over our threshold of patience and tolerance. Be careful not to beat yourself up for slipping back into negative thinking. Instead, cut yourself some slack, acknowledge the stressors that got in your way, and focus your energy on getting back on track.

I suggest continued journaling to help you in this process. For example, write about the challenges you face as well as the successes you encounter. Keeping a log will help you track your progress and recognize the strides you are making, which can be useful when you need some extra encouragement. Be careful not to magnify the obstacles and setbacks while minimizing the gains. Some people find it helpful to form a habit of writing down three positive statements about themselves at the end of each day. Or start your day by writing down or saying an optimistic statement about how your day will go.

Remember the importance of self-care and ensure you are taking time every day to nurture yourself, even if you only have five minutes to spare. The way you treat yourself sends powerful subconscious messages about your perception of your value and worth. Continue adding new ideas to your list of self-care activities as you discover new hobbies and sources of enjoyment.

In *Therapist's Guide to Clinical Intervention: The 1-2-3's of Treatment Planning* (2nd edition), Sharon Johnson says, "You will know that you are developing self-care and self-love when you feel worthy, confident, and secure about who you are." She provides the following demonstrations of progress in self-nurturing:

1.) You spend a day alone and are able to enjoy your own company and peacefulness.

2.) You are able to make choices and do things to make yourself feel better.

3.) You are able to be objective and loyal to yourself. You are able to hear the opinions of others while maintaining your own point of view.

4.)   While you strive to avoid becoming materialistic, you also feel worthy of giving yourself things that are important to you.

5.)   You take care of your health and well-being.

6.)   You do not engage in self-destructive behaviors or choices.

7.)   When you laugh, you laugh deeply and you laugh often.

8.)   You feel good about all of your successes, large and small. You feel good about all that you achieve. You always strive to be the best you can be.

9.)   If someone is rejecting or hurtful, you do not take it personally. You are objective and honest with yourself. You realize that the problem may belong to the other person. Likewise, you are honest with yourself about you, take responsibility, and make changes as needed.

10.)   You are assertive in asking for what you need and want in your relationships with others. You set appropriate boundaries in relationships. [*]

I wish you luck on your lifelong journey to improving self-esteem and creating a healthy, happy life. For more information on any of the topics addressed in this book, please see the References & Recommended Reading listed at the end of the book. Also check out the Resources section on my website, as I am constantly adding new books and resources as I come across them: www.meganmaccutcheon.com/resources

I Am Me[*]
by Virginia Satir

I am me.
In all the world, there is no one else exactly like me.
There are persons who have some parts like me,
but no one adds up exactly like me.
Therefore, everything that comes out of me
is authentically mine because I alone choose it.

I own everything about me
my body, including everything it does;
my mind, including all its thoughts and ideas;
my eyes, including the images of all they behold;
my feelings, whatever they may be
anger, joy, frustration, love, disappointment, excitement;
my mouth, and all the words that come out of it,
polite, sweet or rough, correct or incorrect;
my voice, loud or soft;
and all my actions, whether they be to others or to myself.

I own my fantasies, my dreams, my hopes, my fears.
I own all my triumphs and successes, all my failures and mistakes.

Because I own all of me, I can become intimately acquainted with me.
By so doing I can love me and be friendly with me in all my parts.
I can then make it possible for all of me to work in my best interests.

I know there are aspects about myself that puzzle me,
and other aspects that I do not know.
But as long as I am friendly and loving to myself,
I can courageously and hopefully look for the solutions to the puzzles
and for ways to find out more about me.

However I look and sound, whatever I say and do,
and whatever I think and feel at a given moment in time is me.
This is authentic and represents where I am at that moment in time.

When I review later how I looked and sounded, what I said and did,
and how I thought and felt, some parts may turn out to be unfitting.
I can discard that which is unfitting, and keep that which proved fitting,
and invent something new for that which I have discarded.

I can see, hear, feel, think, say, and do.
I have the tools to survive, to be close to others, to be productive,
and to make sense and order out of the world of people and things outside of me.

I own me, and therefore I can engineer me.

I am me and I am okay.

Recommended Journaling

Wrapping Up

In your journal, write about the various gains you have made as you read through this workbook and completed journaling assignments. What are your biggest accomplishments? What areas do you still need to work on? In what ways do you plan to continue working to build self-esteem?

Are there any topics or areas you feel were not addressed in this workbook regarding your own self-esteem? If so, what are they, and how might you be able to further explore these topics on your own?

15

Assessments Post-Tests

If you filled out the various assessments in previous chapters, you may wish to take them again to see what changes you have made after learning and putting into practice the various tools in this book. After only a few weeks or months, you probably will not do a complete 180, but you will likely notice some shifts in yourself and see some differences in your assessment answers. Your irrational thinking may have decreased slightly or you may be able to cut yourself a break more readily. If you do find some positive differences, give yourself credit for your efforts. If not, keep practicing and remember that breaking long-standing habits takes time.

Rosenberg's Self-Esteem Scale[*]

	Strongly Agree	Agree	Disagree	Strongly Disagree
1.) I feel that I am a person of worth, at least on an equal plane with others.				
2.) I feel that I have a number of good qualities.				
3.) All in all, I am inclined to feel that I am a failure.				
4.) I am able to do things as well as most other people.				
5.) I feel I do not have much to be proud of.				
6.) I take a positive attitude toward myself.				
7.) On the whole, I am satisfied with myself.				
8.) I wish I could have more respect for myself.				
9.) I certainly feel useless at times.				
10.) At times I think I am no good at all.				

Rosenberg's Self-Esteem Scale Scoring:

Scores are calculated as follows:

For items 1, 2, 4, 6, and 7:

Strongly Agree = 3
Agree = 2
Disagree = 1
Strongly Disagree = 0

For items 3, 5, 8, 9, and 10:

Strongly Agree = 0
Agree = 1
Disagree = 2
Strongly Disagree = 3

The scale ranges from 0 – 30. Scores between 15 and 25 are within normal range. Scores below 15 suggest low self-esteem.

The Self-Esteem Review[*]

Directions: Review the following statements. Rate how much you believe each statement, from 1 to 5. The highest rating, 5, means that you think the statement is completely true; 0 means that you completely *do not* believe the statement.

Rating

1.) I am a good and worthwhile person. _____

2.) I am as valuable a person as anyone else. _____

3.) I have good values that guide me in my life. _____

4.) When I look at my eyes in the mirror, I feel good about myself. _____

5.) I feel like I have done well in my life. _____

6.) I can laugh at myself. _____

7.) I like being me. _____

8.) I like myself, even when others reject me. _____

9.) Overall, I am pleased with how I am developing as a person. _____

10.) I love and support myself, regardless of what happens. _____

11.) I would rather be me than someone else. _____

12.) I respect myself. _____

13.) I continue to grow personally. _____

14.) I feel confident about my abilities. _____

15.) I have pride in who I am and what I do. _____

16.) I am comfortable in expressing my thoughts and feelings. _____

17.) I like my body. _____

18.) I handle difficult situations well. _____

19.) Overall, I make good decisions. _____

20.) I am a good friend and people like to be with me. _____

Your total score:

0	100
Total lack of self-esteem	High self-esteem

Mistaken Beliefs Questionnaire*

How much does each of these unconstructive beliefs influence your feelings and behavior? Take your time to reflect about each belief.

      1 = Not so much
      2 = Somewhat / sometimes
      3 = Strongly / frequently
      4 = Very strongly

Place the appropriate number after each statement.

1.)   I feel powerless or helpless.   _____
2.)   Often I feel like a victim of outside circumstances.   _____
3.)   I don't have the money to do what I really want.   _____
4.)   There is seldom enough time to do what I want.   _____
5.)   Life is very difficult—It's a struggle.   _____
6.)   If things are going well, watch out!   _____
7.)   I feel unworthy. I feel that I'm not good enough.   _____
8.)   Often I feel that I don't deserve to be happy or successful.   _____
9.)   Often I feel a sense of defeat and resignation: "Why bother?"   _____
10.)   My condition seems hopeless.   _____
11.)   There is something fundamentally wrong with me.   _____
12.)   I feel ashamed of my condition.   _____
13.)   If I take risks to get better, I'm afraid I'll fail.   _____
14.)   If I take risks to get better, I'm afraid I'll succeed.   _____
15.)   If I felt better, I might have to deal with realities I'd rather not face.   _____
16.)   I feel like I'm nothing (or can't make it) unless I'm loved.   _____
17.)   I can't stand being separated from others.   _____
18.)   If a person doesn't love me in return, I feel like it's my fault.   _____
19.)   It's very hard to be alone.   _____
20.)   What others think of me is very important.   _____
21.)   I feel personally threatened when criticized.   _____
22.)   It's important to please others.   _____
23.)   People won't like me if they see who I really am.   _____
24.)   I need to keep up a front or others will see my weaknesses.   _____
25.)   I have to achieve or produce something significant to feel okay about myself.   _____
26.)   My accomplishments at work/school are extremely important.   _____
27.)   Success is everything.   _____

28.) I have to be the best at what I do. _____

29.) I have to be somebody—somebody outstanding. _____

30.) To fail is terrible. _____

31.) I can't rely on others for help. _____

32.) I can't receive from others. _____

33.) If I let someone get too close, I'm afraid of being controlled. _____

34.) I can't tolerate being out of control. _____

35.) I'm the only one who can solve my problems. _____

36.) I should always be very generous and unselfish. _____

37.) I should always be the perfect:

    a. Employee _____

    b. Professional _____

    c. Spouse _____

    d. Parent _____

    e. Lover _____

    f. Friend _____

    g. Student _____

    h. Son/Daughter _____

38.) I should be able to endure any hardship. _____

39.) I should be able to find a quick solution to every problem. _____

40.) I should never be tired or fatigued. _____

41.) I should always be efficient. _____

42.) I should always be competent. _____

43.) I should always be able to foresee everything. _____

44.) I should never be angry or irritable. _____

45.) I should always be pleasant or nice no matter how I feel. _____

46.) I often feel:

    a. Ugly _____

    b. Inferior or defective _____

    c. Unintelligent _____

    d. Guilty or ashamed _____

47.) I'm just the way I am—I can't really change. _____

48.) The world outside is a dangerous place. _____

49.) Unless you worry about a problem it just gets worse. _____

50.) It's risky to trust people. _____

51.) My problems will go away on their own with time. _____

52.) I feel anxious about making mistakes. _____

53.) I demand perfection of myself. _____

54.) If I didn't have my safe person (or safe place), I'm afraid I couldn't cope. _____

55.) If I stop worrying, I'm afraid something bad will happen. _____

56.) I'm afraid to face the world out there on my own. _____

57.) My self-worth isn't a given—it has to be earned. _____

Mistaken Beliefs Questionnaire Scoring [*]

You may have noticed that some of the beliefs on the questionnaire fall into specific groups, each of which reflects a very basic belief or attitude toward life. (The idea for defining subgroups of beliefs was adapted from David Burns's work.) Go back over your answers and see how you scored with respect to each of the groups of beliefs listed below.

Add your scores for each of the following subgroups of beliefs. If your total score on the items in a particular subgroup exceeds the criterion value, then this is likely to be a problem area for you. It's important that you give this subgroup special attention when you begin to work with affirmations to start changing your mistaken beliefs.

1.) _____	If your total score is over 15: You likely believe that you are powerless, have little or no control over outside circumstances, or are unable to do much that could help your situation. In sum, "I'm powerless" or "I can't do much about my life."
2.) _____	
7.) _____	
9.) _____	
10.) _____	
11.) _____	
TOTAL: ▨	

16.) _____	If your total score is over 15: You likely believe that your self-worth is dependent on the love of someone else. You feel that you need another's (or others') love to feel okay about yourself and to cope. In sum, "My worth and security are dependent on being loved."
17.) _____	
18.) _____	
19.) _____	
54.) _____	
56.) _____	
TOTAL: ▨	

20.) _____	If your total score is over 15: You likely believe that your self-worth is dependent on others' approval. Being pleasing and getting acceptance from others is very important for your sense of security and your sense of who you are. In sum, "My worth and security depend on the approval of others."
21.) _____	
22.) _____	
23.) _____	
24.) _____	
45.) _____	
TOTAL: ▨	

---

[*] The idea for defining subgroups of beliefs was adapted form David Burns, M.D. *Feeling Good.* See his book for future details on how to counter and work with mistaken beliefs.

25.) _____

26.) _____

27.) _____

28.) _____

29.) _____

30.) _____

41.) _____

42.) _____

TOTAL: ░░░░░░

If your total score is over 20: You likely believe that your self-worth is dependent on external achievements, such as school or career performance, status, or wealth. In sum, "My worth is dependent on my performance or achievements."

31.) _____

32.) _____

33.) _____

34.) _____

35.) _____

50.) _____

TOTAL: ░░░░░░

If your score is over 15: You likely believe that you can't trust, rely on, or receive help from others. You may have a tendency to keep a distance from people and avoid intimacy for fear of losing control. In sum, "If I trust or get too close, I'll lose control."

37.) _____

38.) _____

39.) _____

40.) _____

52.) _____

53.) _____

TOTAL: ░░░░░░

If your score is over 25: You likely believe that you have to be perfect in some or many areas of life. You make excessive demands on yourself. There is no room for mistakes. In sum, "I have to be perfect" or "It's not okay to make mistakes."

Survey on Personal Boundaries*

1.) I can't make up my mind.

       Never   Seldom   Occasionally   Often   Usually

2.) I have difficulty saying no to people.

       Never   Seldom   Occasionally   Often   Usually

3.) I feel as if my happiness depends on other people.

       Never   Seldom   Occasionally   Often   Usually

4.) It's hard for me to look a person in the eyes.

       Never   Seldom   Occasionally   Often   Usually

5.) I find myself getting involved with people who end up hurting me.

       Never   Seldom   Occasionally   Often   Usually

6.) I trust others.

       Never   Seldom   Occasionally   Often   Usually

7.) I would rather attend to others than attend to myself.

       Never   Seldom   Occasionally   Often   Usually

8.) Others' opinions are more important than mine.

       Never   Seldom   Occasionally   Often   Usually

9.) People take or use my things without asking me.

       Never   Seldom   Occasionally   Often   Usually

10.) I have difficulty asking for what I want or what I need.

Never   Seldom   Occasionally   Often   Usually

11.) I lend people money and don't seem to get it back on time.

Never   Seldom   Occasionally   Often   Usually

12.) Some people I lend money to don't ever pay me back.

Never   Seldom   Occasionally   Often   Usually

13.) I feel ashamed.

Never   Seldom   Occasionally   Often   Usually

14.) I would rather go along with another person or other people than express what I'd really like.

Never   Seldom   Occasionally   Often   Usually

15.) I feel bad for being so "different" from other people.

Never   Seldom   Occasionally   Often   Usually

16.) I feel anxious, scared, or afraid.

Never   Seldom   Occasionally   Often   Usually

17.) I spend my time and energy helping others so much that I neglect my own wants and needs.

Never   Seldom   Occasionally   Often   Usually

18.) It's hard for me to know what I believe and what I think.

Never   Seldom   Occasionally   Often   Usually

19.) I feel as if my happiness depends on circumstances outside of me.

Never   Seldom   Occasionally   Often   Usually

20.) I feel good.

        Never   Seldom   Occasionally   Often   Usually

21.) I have a hard time knowing what I really feel.

        Never   Seldom   Occasionally   Often   Usually

22.) I find myself getting involved with people who end up being bad for me.

        Never   Seldom   Occasionally   Often   Usually

23.) It's hard for me to make decisions.

        Never   Seldom   Occasionally   Often   Usually

24.) I get angry.

        Never   Seldom   Occasionally   Often   Usually

25.) I don't get to spend much time alone.

        Never   Seldom   Occasionally   Often   Usually

26.) I tend to take on the moods of people close to me.

        Never   Seldom   Occasionally   Often   Usually

27.) I have a hard time keeping a confidence or secret.

        Never   Seldom   Occasionally   Often   Usually

28.) I am overly sensitive to criticism.

        Never   Seldom   Occasionally   Often   Usually

29.) I feel hurt.

        Never   Seldom   Occasionally   Often   Usually

30.) I tend to stay in relationships that are hurting me.

        Never   Seldom   Occasionally   Often   Usually

31.) I feel an emptiness, as if something is missing in my life.

Never Seldom Occasionally Often Usually

32.) I tend to get caught up "in the middle" of other people's problems.

Never Seldom Occasionally Often Usually

33.) When someone I'm with acts up in public, I tend to feel embarrassed.

Never Seldom Occasionally Often Usually

34.) I feel sad.

Never Seldom Occasionally Often Usually

35.) It's not easy for me to really know in my heart about my relationship with a Higher Power or God.

Never Seldom Occasionally Often Usually

36.) I prefer to rely on what others say about what I should believe and do about religious or spiritual matters.

Never Seldom Occasionally Often Usually

37.) I tend to take on or feel what others are feeling.

Never Seldom Occasionally Often Usually

38.) I put more into relationships that I get out of them.

Never Seldom Occasionally Often Usually

39.) I feel responsible for other people's feelings.

Never Seldom Occasionally Often Usually

40.) My friends or acquaintances have a hard time keeping secrets or confidences that I tell them.

Never Seldom Occasionally Often Usually

Boundaries Survey: Assessing and Scoring

In your answers to this survey, many responses of "Usually" and "Often" tend to indicate more boundary problems, distortions, or issues. These may also indicate some confusion over boundaries and limits, often called "blurred" or "fused" boundaries.

Persons who answered all or mostly "Never" may not be aware of their boundaries. A person who has healthy boundaries would tend to answer "Seldom" and sometimes "Occasionally." Rare items, like number 20, would be scored in the reverse.

The Assertiveness Inventory[*]

The following inventory is from *Your Perfect Right: Assertiveness and Equality in Your Life and Relationships* (9th edition) by Robert E. Alberti and Michael L. Emmons. It can help you get an idea of where you stand regarding assertiveness today. Paying attention to difficulties in assertiveness and learning to act more assertively in various situations help to build self-esteem.

Be honest in your responses. All you have to do is draw a circle around the number that describes you best. For some questions, the assertive end of the scale is at 0, for others at 3.

0 = No or Never
1 = Somewhat or Sometimes
2 = Usually or A Good Deal
3 = Practically Always or Entirely

1.) When a person is highly unfair, do you call it to attention?   0 1 2 3

2.) Do you find it difficult to make decisions?   0 1 2 3

3.) Are you openly critical of others' ideas, opinions, behavior?   0 1 2 3

4.) Do you speak out in protest when someone takes your place in line?   0 1 2 3

5.) Do you often avoid people or situations for fear of embarrassment?   0 1 2 3

6.) Do you usually have confidence in your own judgment?   0 1 2 3

7.) Do you insist that your spouse or roommate take on a fair share of household chores?   0 1 2 3

8.) Are you prone to "fly off the handle?"   0 1 2 3

9.) When a salesperson makes an effort, do you find it hard to say no even though the merchandise is not really what you want?   0 1 2 3

10.) When a latecomer is waited on before you are, do you call attention to the situation?   0 1 2 3

11.) Are you reluctant to speak up in a discussion or debate?   0 1 2 3

12.) If a person has borrowed money (or a book, garment, thing of value) and is overdue in returning it, do you mention it?   0 1 2 3

13.) Do you continue to pursue an argument after the other person has had enough?   0 1 2 3

14.) Do you generally express what you feel?   0 1 2 3

15.) Are you disturbed if someone watches you at work?   0 1 2 3

16.) If someone keeps kicking or bumping your chair in a movie or a lecture, do you ask the person to stop?   0 1 2 3

17.) Do you find it difficult to keep eye contact when talking to another person?   0 1 2 3

18.) In a good restaurant when your meal is improperly prepared or served, do you ask the waitperson to correct the situation?   0 1 2 3

19.) When you discover merchandise is faulty, do you return it for an adjustment?   0 1 2 3

20.) Do you show your anger by name-calling or obscenities?   0 1 2 3

21.) Do you try to be a wallflower or a piece of the furniture in social situations?   0 1 2 3

22.) Do you insist that your property manager (mechanic, repairman, etc.) make repairs, adjustments, or replacements which are his/her responsibility?   0 1 2 3

23.) Do you often step in and make decisions for others?   0 1 2 3

24.) Are you able to express love and affection openly?   0 1 2 3

25.) Are you able to ask your friends for small favors or help?   0 1 2 3

26.) Do you think you always have the right answer?　　　0　1　2　3

27.) When you differ with a person you respect, are you able to speak up for your own viewpoint?　　　0　1　2　3

28.) Are you able to refuse unreasonable requests friends make?　　　0　1　2　3

29.) Do you have difficulty complimenting or praising others?　　　0　1　2　3

30.) If someone smoking nearby disturbs you, can you say so?　　　0　1　2　3

31.) Do you shout or use bullying tactics to get others to do as you wish?　　　0　1　2　3

32.) Do you finish other people's sentences for them?　　　0　1　2　3

33.) Do you get into physical fights with others, especially with strangers?　　　0　1　2　3

34.) At family meals, do you control the conversation?　　　0　1　2　3

35.) When you meet a stranger, are you the first to introduce yourself and begin a conversation?　　　0　1　2　3

Analyzing Your Results

Look at individual events in your life involving particular people or groups and consider your strengths and shortcomings accordingly.

Look at your responses to questions 1, 2, 4, 5, 6, 7, 9, 10, 11, 12, 14, 15, 16, 17, 18,19, 21, 22, 24, 25, 27, 28, 30, and 35. These questions are oriented toward nonassertive behavior. Do your answers to these items tell you that you are rarely speaking up for yourself? Or are there perhaps some specific situations that give you trouble?

Look at your responses to questions 3, 8, 13, 20, 23, 26, 29, 31, 32, 33, and 34. These questions are oriented toward aggressive behavior. Do your answers to these questions suggest you are pushing others around more than you realized?

References &
Recommended Reading

Affirmations (Chapter 5):

See Self-Talk / Positive Thinking below

Assertiveness (Chapter 10):

Alberti, R. & Emmons, M. (2008). *Your perfect right: Assertiveness and equality in your life and relationships* (9th ed.). Atascadero, CA: Impact Publishers.

Bloom, L.Z., Corburn, K., & Pearlman, J. (2003). *The new assertive woman: Be your own person through assertive training* (Rev. ed.). Gretna, LA: Selfhelp Success Books.

Bower, S.A. & Bower, G.H. (1991). *Asserting yourself: A practical guide for positive change* (Rev. ed.). Cambridge, MA: Da Capo Press.

Fensterheim, H. & Baer, J. (1975). *Don't say yes when you want to say no.* New York: David McKay Company.

Jakubowksi, P.A. (1977). Self-assertion training procedures for women. In E.I. Rawlings & D.K. Carter (Eds.), *Psychotherapy for women: Treatment toward equality* (pp. 168-190). Springfield, IL: Charles C. Thomas.

Body Image & Eating Issues (Chapter 11):

Johnston, A. (2000). *Eating in the light of the moon: How women can transform their relationships with food through myths, metaphors, and storytelling.* Carlsbad, CA: Gürze Books.

Kilbourne, J. (2010). *Killing us softly 4: Advertising's image of women.* [Documentary film]. Northampton, MA: Media Education Foundation.

Maine, M. (2000). *Body wars: Making peace with women's bodies.* Carlsbad, CA: Gürze Books.

Thompson, K.J. & Cafri, G. (Eds.) (2007). *The muscular ideal: Psychological, social, and medical perspectives.* Washington, DC: American Psychological Association.

Boundaries (Chapter 8):

Whitfield, C.L. (2010). *Boundaries and relationships: Knowing, protecting, and enjoying the self.* Deerfield Beach, FL: Health Communications.

Perfectionism (Chapter 4):

Brown, B. (2013). *Daring greatly: How the courage to be vulnerable transforms the way we live, love, parent, and lead.* New York: Gotham Books.

Brown, B. (2010). *The gifts of imperfection: Let go of who you think you're supposed to be and embrace who you are.* Center City, Minnesota: Hazelden.

Smith, A.W. (2013). *Overcoming perfectionism: Finding the key to balance & self-acceptance* (Rev. and updated). Deerfield Beach, FL: Health Communications.

Self-Care (Chapter 12):

Fontana, D. (1999). *Learn to meditate: A practical guide to self-discovery and fulfillment.* San Francisco, CA: Chronicle Books.

Neff, K. (2011). *Self-compassion: Stop beating yourself up and leave insecurity behind.* New York: Harper Collins.

Schmidt, B. (2014). *The practice: Simple tools for managing stress, finding inner peace, and uncovering happiness.* Deerfield Beach, FL: Health Communications.

Taylor, M. (2008). *Daily om: Inspiration thoughts for a happy, healthy and fulfilling day.* Carlsbad, CA: Hay House.

Self-Esteem (Chapter 2):

Branden, N. (1994). *The six pillars of self-esteem.* New York: Bantam Books.

Burns, D.D. (1993). *Ten days to self-esteem.* New York: HarperCollins.

Hart, L. (2010). *On the wings of self-esteem* (Rev. ed.). Oakland, CA: Uplift Press.

Hay, L.L. (1999). *You can heal your life.* Carlsbad, CA: Hay House.

Loomans, D. (2003). *100 ways to build self-esteem and teach values.* Novato, CA: New World Library.

McKay, M. & Fanning, P. (2000). *Self-esteem: A proven program of cognitive techniques for assessing, improving & maintaining your self-esteem* (3rd ed.). Oakland, CA: New Harbinger Publications.

McKay, M., Fanning, P., Honeychurch, C. & Sutker, C. (1999). *The self-esteem companion: Simple exercises to help you challenge your inner critic and celebrate your personal strengths.* Oakland, CA: New Harbinger Publications.

Schiraldi, G.R (2001). *The self-esteem workbook.* Oakland, CA: New Harbinger.

Self-Esteem & Children (Chapter 13):

Loomans, D. (2003). *100 ways to build self-esteem and teach values.* Novato, CA: New World Library.

Nolte, D. L. & Harris, R. (1998). *Children learn what they live: Parenting to inspire values.* New York: Workman Publishing Company, Inc.

Self-Esteem – Books for Children:

Dyer, W.W. (2005). *Incredible you! 10 ways to let your greatness shine through.* Carlsbad, CA: Hay House.

Hay, L.L. (2008). *I think, I am! Teaching kids the power of affirmations.* Carlsbad, CA: Hay House.

Palmer, P. (2011). *Liking myself.* Weaverville, CA: Boulden Publishing.

Palmer, P. (2011). *The mouse, the monster, and me: Assertiveness for young people.* Weaverville, CA: Boulden Publishing.

Rath, T. & Reckmeyer, M. (2009). *How full is your bucket? For kids.* New York: Gallup Press.

Self-Esteem & Relationships (Chapter 7):

Bloomfield, H. (1996). *Making peace with your parents: The key to enriching your life and all your relationships* (Rev. ed.). New York: Ballantine Books.

Engel, B. (2000). *Loving him without losing you: How to stop disappearing and start being yourself.* New York: John Wiley & Sons.

Self-Talk / Positive Thinking (Chapter 3, 5, 6):

Burns, D.D. (1980). *Feeling good: The new mood therapy.* New York: Harper.

Burns, D.D. (1993). *Ten days to self-esteem.* New York: HarperCollins.

Burns, D.D. (1999). *The feeling good handbook* (Rev ed.). New York: Plume.

Ellis, A. (2001). *Feeling better, getting better, staying better: Profound self-help therapy for your emotions.* Atascadero, CA: Impact Publishers.

Hay, L.L. (1999). *You can heal your life.* Carlsbad, CA: Hay House.

Holden, R. (1998). *Happiness now: Timeless wisdom for feeling good fast.* London: Hodder and Stoughton.

Peale, N.V. (2007). *The power of positive thinking* (Rev. ed.). New York: Fireside.

Satir, V. (1975). *Self-Esteem.* Berkely, CA: Celestial Arts.

Other:

Arden, J.B. (2010). *Rewire your brain: Think your way to a better life.* Hoboken, NJ: John Wiley & Sons.

Bourne, E.J. (2005). *The anxiety & phobia workbook* (4th ed.). Oakland, CA: New Harbinger Publications.

Jacobs, E. (1992). *Creative counseling techniques: An illustrated guide.* Lutz, FL: Psychological Assessment Resources, Inc.

Johnson, S.L. (2004). *Therapist's guide to clinical intervention: The 1-2-3's of treatment planning* (2nd ed.). San Diego, CA: Academic Press.

Megan MacCutcheon, M.Ed., LPC

Megan MacCutcheon, M.Ed., LPC, is a Licensed Professional Counselor (LPC) with a private therapy practice in Vienna, Virginia. Megan provides individual and group therapy to children, adolescents, and adults. Megan specializes in helping individuals to build self-esteem and manage stress, and has extensive experience in working with victims of sexual abuse, emotional abuse, and domestic violence.

Megan also teaches a Building Self-Esteem workshop at The Women's Center (www.thewomenscenter.org), a local nonprofit counseling agency, where she completed an internship and residency, and worked as a therapist and Domestic Violence Systems Advocate.

Megan obtained a Bachelor of Science degree in Communication from Boston University and completed a Master of Education in Counseling and Development at George Mason University. She is a member of the American Counseling Association and Northern Virginia Licensed Professional Counselors.

For more information, please visit www.meganmaccutcheon.com.

Made in the USA
Middletown, DE
12 September 2021